LIVING
THE LITTLE WAY
OF LOVE

John Nelson

LIVING
THE LITTLE WAY
OF LOVE

With
St. Thérèse
of Lisieux

I am alive; yet it is no longer I,
But Christ living in me.
St. Paul

New City
London   New York   Manila

Published in the United States, Great Britain, and the Philippines by
New City Press, 202 Cardinal Rd., Hyde Park, NY 12538
New City, 57 Twyford Avenue, London W3 9PZ and
New City Publications, 4800 Valenzuela St. Sta Mesa, 1016 Manila
www.newcitypress.com

Cover design by Nick Cianfarani
Cover based on a 1881 photo of Saint Thérèse at eight years of age
Original black and white photo from Office Central de Lisieux, V 2 c

Library of Congress Cataloging-in-Publication Data:

Nelson, John, 1931-
      Living the little way of love, with St. Thérèse of Lisieux / John Nelson.
      p. cm.
      Includes bibliographical references.
      ISBN 1-56548-133-X (pbk.)
      1. Thérèse, de Lisieux, Saint, 1873-1897. 2. Spiritual Life--Christianity. I. Title.

BX4700.T5 N45 1999
248.4'82--dc21
                                                                99-050280

1st printing: October 1999
2d printing: December 2000

Printed in Canada

Contents

Acknowledgments

The extracts from Scripture are from *The New Jerusalem Bible,* published and copyright © 1985 by Darton, Longman and Todd Ltd., London, and Doubleday, a division of Bantam Doubleday Dell Publishing Group Inc., New York, and are used by kind permission of the publishers.

The extracts from *Story of a Soul, The Autobiography of St Thérèse of Lisieux,* translated by John Clarke O.C.D., © 1975, 1976 by Washington Province of Discalced Carmelite Friars, Inc., ICS Publications, 2131 Lincoln Road N.E., Washington, D.C. 20002 U.S.A., are used by kind permission of ICS Publications.

The extracts from *St. Thérèse of Lisieux, Her Last Conversations,* translated by John Clarke O.C.D., © 1977 by Washington Province of Discalced Carmelite Friars, Inc., ICS Publications, 2131 Lincoln Road N.E., Washington, D.C. 20002 U.S.A., are used by kind permission of ICS Publications.

The extracts from the *Collected Letters of Saint Thérèse of Lisieux,* translated by F.J. Sheed, © 1949 and published by Sheed and Ward Ltd., London, are used by kind permission of the publishers.

All royalties from sales of this book go to *The Little Way Association,* London, for the purpose of its support and care of missionaries.

Introduction

*My way is all of trust and love, I don't understand souls who
fear so loving a Friend.*

St Thérèse, 9th May 1897

If God be my friend, I cannot be wretched, wrote the poet
Ovid in his *Sorrows*, written in his exile from Rome
occurring within the first two decades of the earthly life
of Jesus Christ. Ovid addressed false gods and was
ignorant of the Hebrew faith in the one true God; but
coincident with Christ's advent, his words written in
perplexity unknowingly anticipate Christian optimism
and hope.

A very few years later, Jesus himself said to his first
disciples, and so to us, 'You are my friends.'[1] He was
encouraging and sustaining the hope of his first
disciples because they were becoming sad and
bewildered as, during the last hours before his arrest,
trial and execution, he told them of his imminent
departure. 'I have told you all this so that you may find
peace in me. In the world you will have hardship, but be
courageous.'[2] At that very moment of perplexity, he
re-assured them that 'your hearts will be full of joy, and
that joy no one shall take from you.'[3] *If God be my friend,
I cannot be wretched.*

This book is about creating an encouraging and
hope-filled friendship with God in a renewed, peaceful
purpose gained in a rightful relationship as his child. It

9

reflects on the truth that encouraging hope and optimistic purpose can be had and held even in a world in which for so many the traditional moral certainties and guidelines fade and fail. *If God be my friend, I cannot be wretched.*

The reader may by chance pick this book up while doubting this God of renewal, but still hoping to chance on some way which makes better sense of the uncertainty through which we all move when living has been adverse. This is a good point from which to begin the journey. Adverse experience is not new for Christians. It was foreseen by Jesus: 'When the Son of Man comes, will he find any faith on earth?' [4] In such times, the Church has been motivated to reform itself, and Christians have been challenged to re-form themselves. These times and experiences make us delve again into our personal objectives and hopes, refine our ways, and find ways to win through. We can again know what (deep, deep down) we knew before — only God knows how to make us happy and able to be candles to lighten darkness. *If God be my friend, I cannot be wretched.*

We have to do this in the detail of our daily life. We do not have the power to act out a Canute-like role, to turn back the tide of events in the world. We have to find our way in and from the *here* and *now*, where we now are. We have to do this amid our many responsibilities and a multitude of things-to-do, with family and friends around us, and so often with little private time. We may have to do it amid troubles caused by failure in any of many aspects of life. We may well feel we cannot do it. But with God all things are possible.[5] So Jesus says to each of us: 'You did not choose me, no, I chose you; and I commissioned you to go out and to bear fruit, fruit that will last.'[6] In the *here* and *now,* and in our littleness and inadequacy in the face of the world, the impossible is promised. *If God be my friend, I cannot be wretched.*

St Thérèse of Lisieux lived the uneventful, ordinary life of an enclosed Carmelite nun in a small provincial French town in the late years of the nineteenth century. She was a nun for a mere nine years, calmly and heroically meeting a painful death at the age of twenty-four years. Her companions within this strict enclosure numbered little more than two dozen, and many of them never recognized anything so very highly special about her, though they saw that she was a good religious, with a robust and lively sense of humour and with constant common sense, living faithfully according to the Carmelite Rule. However, within a very few decades she became one of the most loved of all the saints. It is only little more than a century ago that she discovered 'a short, direct, new way' to spiritual fulfilment and fruitfulness: a little way available to everyone in any state and walk of life. She stated that Jesus alone had given her this inspiration. In his earthly ministry he had urged us to become as little children. Thérèse understood that little children cannot perform great deeds but can and do give great love. She had learned from St John of the Cross that love is repaid by love alone. So she confidently pursued the little way of love of a child of God, saying that everything she did in this way must be possible for any ordinary person like herself. Most of us share with her that hidden-ness and unknown-ness which she took as a gift of God. Through him she turned it triumphantly into a rich spiritual experience, to the benefit and encouragement now of millions of people. Her little way is one of deep, utterly trusting friendship with God. *If God be my friend, I cannot be wretched.*

Thérèse's way of coming close to God and of reflecting him into the world is very apt for our times. It is singularly suited to the lives of those of us who live in the secular world and find our livings, activities and interests in the company of many who do not have meaningful belief in God. The little way is devoid of extraordinary penances or asceticism, it teaches no fixed method of prayer, it is absent of any aspirations to extraordinary mystical experiences, and it eschews dependence on numerous exterior good works. It is a way of fruitful little means, without ostentation or exaggerated pretensions; a way of littleness and hiddeness. It is a direct, short way to spiritual health and to the fullness of the life of God within us. The little way is a way of integration, involvement and community through love. The little way is holistic—better, wholistic—with a unity of simple parts, as perceived by the author, which can be expressed as;

1. **joyful humility** as a little child of God,

2. **bold confidence** in God's mercy and loving-kindness,

3. **tranquil trust** in the actions of God's limitless love,

4. **persistence in prayer** as a simple raising of the heart to God,

5. **daily practice** of the little way of love.

The little way of love leads to that spiritual wholeness to which we are all called by Jesus when he says, 'You must therefore set no bounds to your love, just as your heavenly Father sets none to his.' [7]

The little way is for action, not for uninvolved admiration. This book is a practical exploration of Thérèse's inspiration — the *what, why and how* of her ideas considered in the context of our ordinary daily life. Within a Scriptural context, and in an ecumenical light, it draws on some supportive relevant experiences of God in different Christian traditions, and from our own and previous centuries. The purpose is to encourage and assist the reader in the daily practice of the little way of love. It is a volume which can act as companion to my previous book, *Into the Arms of Love with St. Thérèse of Lisieux* (Darton, Longman and Todd, London, 1997; published in 1998 in the United States of America by Liguori Publications, Missouri, under the title *The Little Way of Saint Thérèse of Lisieux*) in which the reader will find the above listed core elements of the little way introduced with readings from the sayings and writings of Thérèse set in a context of related extracts from Scripture and *The Imitation of Christ*, for daily reflection and encouragement.

No two lives are the same and each of us will find Jesus as a Friend in that unique way which he wills for each; but if Jesus has truly been encountered it is always in an ending of subjectivity and in the advent of fruitfulness. Thérèse's profound insights are for all (whatever their particular beliefs, circumstance or conditions) inspiring optimism and hope in renewed purpose in a world in need of the Way of Jesus. *With God as my Friend, then I cannot be wretched.*

Chapter 1

Prologue

*Summary of the little way
drawn from the words of St Thérèse*

JOYFUL HUMILITY AS A LITTLE CHILD OF GOD
The little child expects everything from God
as a child expects everything from its father.
Knowing that it is weak and little,
in humility the child seeks to become more and more so.
The child is not discouraged over its faults,
and is disquieted about nothing,
for children fall often but are too little
to hurt themselves very much.
The child knows it is incapable of making its living,
and can be raised to heaven only in Jesus' arms.

**BOLD CONFIDENCE IN GOD'S MERCY
AND LOVING-KINDNESS**
The little child knows that God
is more tender than any mother.
Love penetrates and surrounds the child
in the eternal embrace of merciful loving-kindness.
The child knows that the faults of his child
do not cause God any pain;
love will quickly consume everything,

leaving only a profound peace and joy of heart.
In Jesus' arms, never discouraged,
the child is launched on waves of love and bold confidence.

TRANQUIL TRUST IN THE ACTIONS
OF GOD'S LIMITLESS LOVE

The little child knows that Jesus acts within it,
inspiring it in all he desires it to do at each moment.
Following the way of confidence and total abandon,
it is happy only to do the will of God.
Knowing that it is Jesus' hand that governs all,
in everything the child sees only Jesus,
knowing that it is trust and nothing but trust
that will bring it to love
and that God does not disappoint a trust
so filled with humility.

PERSISTENCE IN PRAYER
AS A SIMPLE RAISING OF THE HEART TO GOD

The little child says very simply to God
what the child wishes to say;
and is persistent in raising the heart
and simple glances towards heaven
in a cry of love and gratitude
in the midst of trial as well as in joy.
The child never grows weary of praying,
with a confidence which works miracles,
because everything that it asks of its Father
in Jesus' name will be granted.

DAILY PRACTICE OF THE LITTLE WAY OF LOVE

The little child knows that Jesus does not demand great actions
but simply surrender and gratitude,
and that the smallest act of pure love is of more value
than all other works put together.
The child is content to be empty handed,
not asking for its works to be counted,
but doing everything for love,
refusing Jesus nothing,
with the one purpose of pleasing and consoling Jesus,
giving joy to Jesus.

Then Jesus,
who loves the child even to folly,
does everything for the little one,
for He would not inspire
the longings of the child
unless He wanted to grant them.
Jesus alone
can fulfil immense desires.

Chapter 2

Joyful humility as a little child of God

It is to recognize our nothingness, to expect everything from God as a little child expects everything from its father; it is to be disquieted about nothing, and not to set on gaining our living . . . it is not to become discouraged over one's faults, for children fall often, but they are too little to hurt themselves very much.

St Thérèse, 6th August 1897, said while explaining what she meant by remaining a little child before God.

In the cool of the evening Nicodemus brooded over the teaching of the Rabbi he had come to hear after the activity and heat of the day. As descending darkness shrouded the landscape so familiar to him, he pondered the enigmatic sayings of this Teacher to whom he felt strangely drawn. The words rang with significance and power — but they were also very puzzling. Well-known certainties, and even common sense itself, were being challenged.

Nicodemus was a learned and clever man, one of the faithful Pharisees who numbered only some several thousand in the whole nation of Israel, respected by the

Chosen People, leading them in a strict adherence to
God's covenant with them. He struggled in his
knowledge and sophistication with the seeming
implication of some sort of return to a child's state, in
Jesus' teaching of the necessity of being born from
above, being born again. 'How can anyone who is
already old be born? Is it possible to go back into the
womb again and be born?' he wondered.[1] How can
anyone be born twice?

The words of the Rabbi, Jesus, were: 'In all truth I tell
you [this solemn phrase introduces Jesus' most
significant sayings, to underline their fundamental
nature], no one can see the kingdom of God without
being born from above . . . no one can enter the
kingdom of God without being born through water and
the Spirit. . . . You must be born from above.'[2] This text
is the basis of our belief in Christian baptism, enabling
a new life lived in the Holy Spirit. We can also relate it
to the teaching given on another occasion when Jesus
again stresses the imperative need for radical renewal, a
spiritual rebirth: 'In truth I tell you, unless you change
and become like little children you will never enter the
kingdom of Heaven. And so, the one who makes
himself as little as this little child is the greatest in the
kingdom of Heaven.'[3]

It is worthwhile for a moment staying with these
words. You will not see the kingdom of God without
being born from above, or—as some translations of the
Bible have it — being born again. Unless you change
and become like a little child you will never enter the
kingdom of heaven. The one who makes himself as

little as a very little child is the greatest in the kingdom of heaven.

We who perhaps are so used to these words on being born from above, or born again can easily wonder at the puzzlement of a sophisticated spiritual leader of the people chosen by God to be his means to reveal himself to the world. We are familiar with the event of baptism. Indeed, for those who do not find their way to church too often other than at christenings, weddings and funerals, it may become merely a pleasant social custom or a simple membership ceremony rather than a radical religious event. Even those of us who do make the effort to get to church easily overlook the fact that at each and every baptism the earth moves and the heavens open. Similarly, we have long lived with the sayings about the little children, for Jesus spoke several times on this theme. They are overlaid in our minds with images of little, trusting ones clustered innocently round the shepherd Lord. It is a pleasant thought that Jesus also loved little children. We are accustomed, we are so used to these words of Jesus; we cease to really listen. We may not see their fundamental impact. We so easily overlook the fact that Jesus speaks these words to each of us, to each one of us. He is challenging our familiar certainties, and even what we often regard as common sense.

An imperative, not an option

'Therefore, everyone who listens to these words of mine and acts on them will be like a sensible man who built his house on rock.'[4] Jesus' words require real attention. In truth, he is giving to us an imperative condition, not an option. It is not that Jesus will *also* care for little children, but rather I must become like a little child. I must undergo a re-generation, be born again from above.

Jesus teaches us that we must be, not like little children as in some pretty but superficial imitation, but that we must *change and become as* little children. Suddenly, if we really listen to Jesus, all the aura of unchanging comfortable resort which religion seems normally to offer has evaporated. Instead, the challenge of radical change is placed before us. We must return to our real beginning to realize our true end.

Children are unable and are utterly dependent upon their parent. Literally, *we* must become helpless, totally provided for, shorn of means and ability. We must become spiritually poverty-stricken. The image changes — it is no longer one of attractive docility. It may even be felt as threatening and revolution-ary — that is to say, to fulfil this command we need to revolve, turn around, until we see from another direc-tion all that about which up to now we have made assumptions; and at which we have not looked really closely and clearly because it has been long with us and not given much thought or attention.

The image changes from that of the innocent young clustered round the Lord with us as admiring onlookers, to that of the radically changed and reduced finding their way back to him.

All fundamental change seems threatening because we are challenged to go somewhere for which we do not have any maps. We love to know where we are going, we love to take charge of things. We have been taught all our lives to become adults. Adults take responsibility. Adults are in charge. All children want to become adults — that is only reasonable. Why else are they children?

The required change is so great that to achieve it is tantamount to being made anew in our seeing and in our mind. It is like being re-generated, born again. We speak, do we not, about a new idea or development being borne in on one when it becomes one's conviction? We say, 'A new idea was born . . .' It comes to us as such a challenge that we either reject it and childishly refuse to explore new possibilities, or we nod sagely and lose the sharp point in sophisticated verbiage, or we go with it and can end by saying, in the excitement of discovery of new horizons: 'Ah, *now* I see! . . .' Then there is a pleasure, a joy in this new prospect. We have found some aspect of the dearest freshness deep down things and morning, at the brown brink eastward, springs — to express it in the words of Gerard Manley Hopkins.

All change is a challenge, and we, in our familiar, adult certainties have learned to overcome such challenges very cleverly. We have learned ways and means, become sophisticated and able to do so. Much of contemporary good management technique is intended to emphasize the adroit management of change in a period of deep changes in commerce and industry. Such practice is intended to enable the people subject to change to accept it and to feel that the sting has been taken out of the challenge of change.

We pride ourselves on our achievements in managing in the face of the challenge of life. We are certainly not averse to others knowing about them. With Christian belief, or with its remnants still with us in our culture, we remember that we are supposed to avoid boasting. But the evidence of our success in overcoming the challenges of life is seen by others, it is on display. We cannot avoid that, can we? That's not wrong, surely, because it shows others that with the same efforts they can do it as well. We like to encourage others to have the same success in managing and measuring up to life. And even if the appearance of success is not really true, we keep up appearances and make it seem so. Our self-esteem, our pride requires that. Life has not succeeded in breaking us, we've managed somehow. It seems reasonable to be proud of that. We may even sometimes remember to attribute our success to God-given talents.

Or, some of us feel defeated by our failures to measure up to these challenges of life and we hide our shame. We don't seem to have much to say for ourselves. We've lost our pride. We are hurt, damaged. We feel perplexed and broken. But, what is broken can be mended. What is unbroken has to be broken to be mended. The perplexity, the breaking, the loss of self-pride, may be a gift, a Godsend?

False pride, the product of the Fall

Pride comes before a fall may seem an old, worn-out adage—but certainly, a false self-pride came before the Fall. Is, then, the God who arranged this world of ours the Great Breaker in the sky? It would be unreasonable to think so, for we ourselves build the hurdle of our own pride when we do things of ourselves, with such emphasis upon self. Self-pride such as we often have was not part of the original scheme of things.

So much of our contemporary competitive, acquisitive society, for all its many essential benefits and blessings, creates conditions of emphasis upon self and self-pride. From the communal, shared deprivation for many in previous times, we in the West have moved to the wealthiest civilization of all time and to an emphasis upon the satisfaction of self. As a product of this there is for many a growth of the consequent aloneness of much modern life. Despite our rightful efforts to provide through the State community, we seem to destroy the essential element of true community. For an increasing number of us, apparently, the result is suffering in isolation. So in our social building and activity for the satisfaction of needs we also create deeper need which is not met and answered by our material society. The casualties of pride and independence abound, and they do not include only those who are the obviously wounded. An unbalanced emphasis upon self is open increasingly to questioning. Is there, keeping what is good, another way?

We need again to look at a way that is revolutionary—that is, we need to revolve, turn around until we see with fresh sight from another direction that about which we have made assumptions and become very used. Revolution has a bad name in our political experience. It is a political means to force the opinions of some onto all. It is the political use of power to manage others at their painful cost. But religious revolution, Jesus, is not of this world and does not use the powers of this world.[5] His revolution begins not in the national State but in the personal state. As Paul commented, our minds must be renewed in a spiritual revolution so that we can put on the new self that has been created in God's way.[6]

Mother Teresa says she began her revolutionary rescuing of her forsaken children not in terms of thousands but in one. But to do this she had first to leave and lose what she had in her former well-provided convent life and go out alone to a place where she had nothing and where simple faith stood in place of any certain knowledge of the future. Then the miracle happened. The one became the many. Starting from that one first step, the world will never be the same again.

We must begin realistically where we are, in ourselves. We must begin in a way that is authenticated by each of us, in us; in a way which is the Way, the Truth and Life.[7] Then starting from the One, we can change the world round us, we can give to it. We cannot give to the world what we do not have. We must gain in order to give. We cannot gain until we have lost.

Loss, then gain, then giving. Then the one can become the many.

How much I have to lose!

The gift which Thérèse shares with us is her ability to look afresh at that which is already known but of which we have lost the clear sight, the sharp perspective, in a blur of custom and familiarity. Then in direct, clear words and concrete imagery she tells us what she has seen so that the sight of others is refreshed. One day Thérèse was approached by her sister Céline who was feeling discouraged amid difficulties in her early days as a nun. How much, said Céline, I have yet to acquire! No, replied Thérèse, say rather—*how much I have to lose!*[8]

Many of us have to begin from the loss we may experience in our present daily life; from disruption and suffering, from whatever cause. That can be an advantage, for revolution begins from unsettlement and often from distress. We need to be unsettled. John the Baptist came from the desert to unsettle the settled, to wash the unwashed, to clear a way to new life. Jesus came after to teach us that we have to lose our life to gain our life. A grain of wheat must die in the dark ground to spring into new life and grow towards the light to yield a rich harvest.[9] If we are already in the dark ground we have made a start. That is the good news; the Gospel amidst loss. Our perplexity is then a symptom which can create the urge to find a doctor and a cure. That is the Godsend: symptoms are good because they reveal injury and disease. They open our eyes to what is real, the fundamental need. Then we can be like Thérèse who saw through the eyes of a child discovering a world of renewal and fresh hope.

We are easily broken, but we cannot easily mend ourselves. The truth is, we find it so often impossible to mend ourselves that we make do as best we can. We make do — and mend if and when we can. We avoid uncomfortable revolutionary discoveries which might make things even more unstable; so often, we would simply like to find out how to get through from one end of life to the other without too many (or, so many) mishaps. We avoid the inconvenient.

But, inconveniently, here is Jesus insisting that unless we *change* and become like *little* children we will never enter the kingdom of heaven. He radically cuts across so much of our contemporary thinking and ways of organizing life. His requirement is not of this world. But the world cannot be right with heaven until so changed. There is an imperative for radical change in its relationship and in our relationships. We ourselves cannot mend and change ourselves so radically. We cannot of ourselves turn our world so upside down, nor see our successes and failures so in reverse that what was gained is seen as loss and what was seen as loss is really gain. Our inability is palpable and perplexing.

We need renewed eyes to see that we must totally, utterly, profoundly rely upon only him who demands such radical, such unnatural change of us. We need the eyes of a child to look and learn again. The world needs to see again with eyes as they were at its birth in creation when Adam's new eyes were first opened onto light and wonder. And the world will not go where we have not first been so that then we can, like Thérèse and Mother Teresa, tell concretely and clearly what we have seen so that the sight of others is also refreshed and made new.

Jesus' imperative is revolutionary. He asks it of us but we ourselves cannot do it of ourselves, for we carry with us the damage caused by Adam's first fit of self-pride. So Jesus must do it for us. But how?

Without means to pay nor able to earn

He invites us to 'come to the water all you who are thirsty; though you have no money, come! Buy and eat; come, buy wine and milk without money, free!'[10] They do not have money-changers in heaven, for they were whipped by Jesus out of the Temple. Heaven has only people-changers, the saints such as Thérèse . . . and unknown saints such as we will be when we have been challenged, and failed of ourselves and so been forced to follow blindly but faithfully to an unseen end, enabled with goods for which we neither have means to pay nor are able to earn.

In birth, a child loses the warm, enclosing security of the womb and is ejected into that which it does not know. Birth is something done to it, not by it. First comes the loss, and only then the gain. After losing its previous repose in the womb, the child is washed. The traces of its previous place have to be stripped from it. Only then is it reclothed. Loss, unknowing, stripping, reclothing, gain—in that order. This all happens to the child in its helplessness and inability. It cannot even see as it travels with closed eyes, and it cannot see clearly as it arrives in a new place for its eyes are not used to this new world. Only later, as it learns within the guidance and example of others, from whom it has trustingly to receive all, does the child gain clear sight; and only later still, full understanding. That comes last, and we are blessed indeed if we reach it. Before this fruition, there has to be complete faith and trust; their fruitfulness is realized within an unknowing — the trusting blindness, inability, dependency and helplessness of the child.

Going from *here* to *there* requires demolition, radical movement, a departure, change. Jesus said, 'Unless you change. . . .' I must be stripped before being re-clothed, as a child is stripped, washed and re-clothed. I can do nothing for myself. The stripping will be painful if I resist and twist and turn as does an unwilling child; one who behaves, as we say, child*ishly*. C.S. Lewis has commented that pain plants the flag of truth in a rebel fortress. In contrast, I must be child*like* and depend upon, trust in, another to do all for me. Then the pain abates as the relationship becomes right, and true, and real. Forgiveness, Jesus' giving for me, is a two-way process; as Jesus seeks and unsettles me and gives himself for me, I need to accept his giving. In accepting his forgiveness, I leave unsettlement and give myself to him. Of one thing I can be sure, the Saviour who died in agony for me, who has bought and paid for me, will rightly not leave me in peace and settlement while I try to go on a way that ignores him. There is no peace

outside his peace. While unsettlement and pain are not
in themselves good, they have a certain relative good if
they are means to bring me to my true life in Jesus. I can
yet live to bless my experience of loss and even pain.
Jesus knows better than I do the terrible cost of a choice
by me to remain ever outside his peace.

The diagnosis and the healing

Jesus said that if anyone loves his life, he will lose it.[11]
He was not being threatening nor repressive, his words
are not judgmental; instead, they are both a diagnosis
and a healing. He simply reflected on the fact of our
nature as creatures, children of God. He was being
reasonable in describing the result of the action of the
dependent child which turns away from its parent and
towards itself in its self-wilfulness. Surely, centredness
upon self is sterile, and self-defeating to the point of
pain and a living death. Even in a living death our
self-regard and pride can still self-destructively urge us
to look inwards and to refuse the rescue which comes
upon us from outside our own false centre. 'How often
have I longed to gather your children together, as a hen
gathers her chicks under her wings, and you refused!'[12]
But he also said, anyone who loses his life will find
it—if they seek it in him.[13] First comes loss; then comes
gain, the fruit of loss.

Jesus told St. Catherine of Siena: *I am*, you are not.
Scripture tells of us: Look, you are less than
nothingness, and what you do is less than nothing.[14]
'The moment he sees us convinced of our nothingness,

he reaches out his hand: if we still want to try some great thing, even under colour of zeal, the good Jesus leaves us to ourselves,' wrote Thérèse.[15] To be, I must be endlessly helpless that he may do all for me. Then all is Jesus; there is no other. This perishable nature of mine must put on imperishability, this mortal nature put on immortality,[16] not to live for myself anymore but to be alive in him who raises me to life.[17] Then I am real-*ized* by and in Jesus. We have a saying among younger people nowadays — be real!, they say. It is an imperative, not an option. It is about being honest and facing facts. Religion, like politics (they both are concerned with things which affect us fundamentally) easily produces make-believe stances. But we must be real and face the facts.

Our luminosity is entirely of God

Given, then, that we must become little children, our incorrigible precocity and pride continually urges us to move from being little children — who are, of course, endlessly dependent — to some further state where we can earn our living and contribute our pennyworth. We feel that we are called to stand on our own feet. We feel that we must make ourselves somehow worthy, or at least worthier, in the eyes of God. Our inheritance from Adam leads us into the trap of thinking that while it is accepted that the first move comes from God, we are called and able to accept the gift of his love as our Creator and then multiply the gift so that it can be returned, worthily, to God. After all, did he not tell us to be good stewards of his talents? Well then, we shall set to work to use those God-given talents and do good with them. God will then be pleased with us, he will then love us and we will deserve his rewards. In his discussion of *The Four loves*, C. S. Lewis wrote:

> No sooner do we believe that God loves us than there is an impulse to believe that he does so, not because he is Love, but because we are intrinsically loveable . . . Far be it from us to think that we have virtues for which God could love us. But then, how magnificently we have repented! . . . Thus, depth beneath depth and subtlety within subtlety, there remains some lingering idea of our own, our very own, attractiveness. It is easy to acknowledge, but almost impossible to realize for long, that we are mirrors whose brightness, if we are bright, is wholly derived from the Sun that shines upon us. Surely we must have a little — however little—native luminosity? Surely we can't be *quite* creatures?[18]

We are creatures, but free creatures. If we choose to remain darkened, we can. We were given freedom, called free will. We can say 'no'. But there is no *rational* reason or cause for us to do so. God does everything to bring us to him, from wherever we have wandered in our misuse of the gift of freedom. Nothing is impossible to God, and he does have ways and means to lead us finally to accept that our light is wholly derived from him. He is very intent upon us. It must be said that his ways and means may seem disturbing, but the pain is *not* caused by him. When I cease misusing my freedom, and turn, revolve, evolve to him, the pain abates in the fresh use of my atrophied spiritual capacity, passing into a correct relationship with God. Jesus said, 'Cut off from me, you can do nothing.'[19] 'Jesus does everything, I nothing', wrote Thérèse.[20]

So, to make sense of my experiences in life, I need to capitulate into a rightful, natural relationship with God as his child. The converse of my fruitlessness outside my natural and rightful relationship with God is that, with Jesus, anything good can be done. As St Paul said, 'There is nothing I cannot do in the One who strengthens me.'[21] But, beware. It is Jesus, and Jesus alone who does it for me. Anything which suggests anything remotely else is simply the subtly of the serpent. To slip under the coils of the serpent without him seeing, I must be very, very little. Daringly, Thérèse went so far as to say, 'As for me, I have lights only to see my little nothingness. This does me more good than all the lights on the faith.'[22] I must, then, be stripped and go before God naked, offering my nothingness and inability. Thérèse spoke about this state of total dependency in a letter to her sister Céline: 'We must number ourselves humbly with the imperfect, see ourselves as little souls which God must uphold from instant to instant. . . . Let us take each other's hand and run to the last place, no one will dispute with us.' She had previously noted: 'The one thing that is not envied is the last place; the last place is the one thing that is not vanity and affliction of spirit.'[23]

We do not go to God from our goodness, or good works. We can only give ourselves as we are. We go to him in our imperfectness. The rest is his business. We ought not to even watch him working in us, but just trust and know that he has welcomed us and will do all for us.

Our incapacity is our qualification for heaven

This story from the fourth century AD hermit monks of the deserts of the Middle East relates to our discussion:

> They said of Abbot Pambo that in the very hour when he departed this life he said to the holy men who stood by him — From the very time I came to this place in the desert, and built me a cell, and dwelt here, I do not remember eating bread that was not earned by the work of my own hands, nor do I remember saying anything for which I was sorry even until this hour. And thus I go to the Lord as one who has not even made a beginning in the service of God.[24]

We go to God in our lack of earning capacity and in lack of things correctly said and done. Our incapacity is our blessed and glorious qualification for heaven. It is our ticket to ride — in the power of Jesus, in his arms.

The point being made by Abbot Pambo about the error of seeking achievement through self-reliance was also dealt with by Thérèse when she was talking to her sister Pauline, Mother Agnes of Jesus, explaining what she meant by *remaining a little child before God*. Thérèse explained that she prayed for preservation from proud thoughts, and went on to say:

> If I were to say to myself: I have acquired a certain virtue, and I am certain I can practice it, this would be relying upon my own strength, and when we do this we run the risk of falling into the abyss. However, I will have the right of doing stupid things up until my death, if I am humble and I remain little. Look at little children: they never stop breaking things, tearing things, falling down, and they do this even while loving their parents very, very much. When I fall in this way, it makes me realize my nothingness more, and I say to myself: What would I do, and what would I become, if I were to rely upon my own strength?
>
> I understand very well why Saint Peter fell. Poor Peter, he was relying upon himself instead of relying only upon God's strength. I conclude from this experience that if I said to myself: 'O my God, You know very well I love You too much to dwell upon one single thought against the faith,' my temptations

would become more violent and I certainly would succumb to them.

I am very sure that if Saint Peter had said humbly to Jesus: 'Give me the grace, I beg You, to follow You even to death,' he would have received it immediately.

I'm very certain that Our Lord didn't say any more to His apostles through His instructions and His physical presence than He says to us through His good inspirations and his grace. He could have said to Saint Peter: 'Ask Me for the strength to accomplish what you want.' But no, He didn't because He wanted to show him his weakness, and because, before ruling the Church that is filled with sinners, he had to experience for himself what man is able to do without God's help.

Before Peter fell, Our Lord had said to him: 'And once you are converted, strengthen your brethren.'[25] This means: Convince them of the weakness of human strength through your own experience.[26]

Thérèse applies her gift of looking afresh through new eyes at what is already seemingly known. She sees the great spiritual significance of the very ordinary, commonplace tasks and happenings of our daily life, and sees these transfused, if we but quietly and trustingly allow it, with God's search and action for us. When we are little enough to know our complete weakness and so rely only on him, he who is All makes himself little that he may enter us and enable us, through and in his strength. From our own poverty, we gain all his riches. But they remain always his, to be used only in him. Without him, we do nothing.

A psychological and spiritual treasure

The spirituality of littleness allows us at last to relate to God everything which happens to us in the ordinary course of events, even our pains, faults and failures. Thérèse commented that she did not always succeed in rising above the nothings of this earth, those many small discouraging occasions when we, like St Paul, do what we would not do and do not do what we would do: 'For example, I will be tormented by a foolish thing I said or did. Then I enter into myself, and I say: Alas, I am still at the same place as I was formerly! But I tell myself this with great gentleness and without any sadness! It's so good to feel that one is weak and little!'[27] The little way is at least a way to cope with our failures and seeming inability, preventing despondency and despair, removing the infliction and pain of ourselves. If it were no more than that, it would be a psychological and spiritual treasure.

Nothing is too little to contain him, and to be the means of being with him, of obtaining his gifts, and so sharing his work. His divine action is in every event of daily life and they become thereby the means by which we are graced and so enabled to co-operate with him as he draws us to him and we become fully real-ized in him. Without him, we are shadows, unreal, unrealized. With him we become heirs to his Kingdom. It is children who are heirs, and who gain all that belongs to the parent. From nothingness we pass to full being. From poverty and inability we pass to infinite riches. But always his is the hand which feeds the child which remains content in its childhood and utter dependency.

Thérèse's forerunner in the understanding of the rich spiritual significance of the ordinary events in ordinary life, Jean-Pierre de Caussade, expressed it thus:

> Yes, dear Love, all souls would reach supernatural, sublime, wonderful, inconceivable heights, if they would all be content with thy action! Yes, indeed, if we could only allow this divine hand to act, we should reach the most eminent perfection! All would reach it for it is offered to all. All we have to do is open our mouths, as it were, and perfection will enter of itself . . . it would not be necessary for them to copy each other; the divine action would *individualize each one of them by the most ordinary methods*.[28]

Of those who depart from self-reliance and are open and unresisting, de Caussade also says:

> The Holy Spirit . . . writes his own gospel, and he writes it in the hearts of the faithful.[29]

A gospel is the good news of Jesus told by the Holy Spirit. We are the paper upon which that good news can be written if we will. We should not be conscious of the letters, but others may read them and be lifted up. The saints are not distinguished by their regard for their own goodness, but by their honest recognition of their complete need, their sinful state. Sin is not a positive thing — it is a negative, an emptiness, a need which can only be filled by God, not by ourselves. Nor are saints carbon-copies of each other turned out on some common celestial pattern. We may be inspired by one as an exemplar, but we each have our own special gifts from God, each our own special relationship with him. We are all of a rich, infinite variety which will be our joy when all is consummated and we finally reach heaven. That is why we should not make assumptions nor hold to stereotypes. Let God write as he wishes in me and let me be content not to peep over his shoulder. If we accept our dependency he is able to be patient and gentle with us, making the footprints into which our steps can be placed and by the outline of which we can know he is here, even in our pains and distress, which he shares with us to their end. Then, even in their midst, we are surprised by joy, as joy over new life floods in after the pangs of birth.[30]

Goodwill alone is sufficient

Thérèse passed through several painful crises in her life. She knew much suffering. Her holiness was not gained in a field of flowers, in a pastoral delight devoid of hurt. She lost her mother through death by cancer at the age of four and a half years. She loved her mother dearly and the wound went very deep. From having been a lively, open and cheerful child she became diffident and over-sensitive. After choosing her older sister Pauline as her second 'mother', she found herself orphaned again at the age of nine years when Pauline left home to enter religious life: Thérèse's tears were bitter, and in the following protracted illness she describes herself as having apparently lost her reason. Her sister Marie became her third 'mother.' Yet again, at thirteen years of age, she was deprived of Marie, her 'last support', who departed to the convent. Thérèse then became withdrawn and in her distress became almost unbearable in her touchiness and childish reaction to the ordinary disappointments of daily life. It was not until the Christmas before her fourteenth birthday that she experienced what she describes as 'a little miracle to make me grow up in an instant . . . he made me strong and courageous.' She describes herself as then leaving her childhood (this is important for any who imagine that her teaching of being a little child before God is some form of prettified psychological regression into an infantile spirituality) in the grace of a complete conversion.

> The work I had been unable to do in ten years was done by Jesus in one instant, contenting Himself with my good will which was never lacking. I could say to Him like His apostles: 'Master, I fished all night and caught noth-ing.'[31] More merciful to me than He was to His disciples, Jesus took the net Himself, cast it, and drew it in filled with fish . . . I felt charity

(*fruitful outreaching love*) enter my soul, and the
need to forget myself and please others; since
then I've been happy![32]

Always Thérèse stresses that the way she has
discovered is a way for all little people; ordinary people
like herself, as she put it. She was intent on doing
nothing which could not be done by any of the
multitude with whom she identified herself, and to
whom she returns to assist them along the little way.
She was healed in an instant, she tells us. Our healing
can be as speedy, but we must want it and we should
ask for it, as dependent children ask. Without Jesus we
can at most reach some sort of stoic resignation. He
promises and does infinitely more.

Following this Christmas miracle she presses forward
and, having received from God in her sheer and urgent
need, she then decides to ask for more. Not some little
thing which he would hardly notice, but a great thing.
Little souls need many great things given them because
they have nothing of their own. Thérèse sets to and
asks God for the salvation of a criminal condemned to
the guillotine for a horrible murder. Sure enough, her
prayers were answered to the letter. Going to the
scaffold having spurned all the religious aid offered him
in the previous days, the criminal turned from placing
his head on the block and suddenly asked for a crucifix
and kissed the sacred wounds three times. Then calmly
he went to his death and salvation. For us, so often
having to seek a way to cope with life's daily arrows and
misfortunes, the important part of Thérèse's narrative

is her reaction to the signs of God's care and his involvement with her concerns:

> God was able in a very short time to extricate me from the very narrow circle in which I was turning without knowing how to come out. When seeing the road He made me travel, my gratitude was great; but I must admit, if the biggest step was taken, there remained many things for me to leave behind.[33]

Thérèse has been released from the prison of herself. Her release was done *to* her, *for* her. She simply returned gratitude, seeing the way ahead through the sight then given her. In this release she immediately thought of, and worked for, others who were still in the prison of themselves. Her release is itself a sign of the further road to be travelled in the movement from self. Nothing is more painful than fixation upon self. The constant turning over of the problems and pains in this close encirclement is wearying and adds pain. As soon as Thérèse is released she travels; immediately she starts, she takes company with her. Such release is always in a movement which immediately encompasses others. It is a release from self-centredness, to other-centredness which of itself moves attention to others around us. It is paralleled by the sending out by Jesus of the seventy-two disciples in pairs, saying to them, 'Start off now, but look, I am sending you out like lambs among wolves. Take no purse with you, no haversack, no sandals . . .' All each had was the

company of the other. But they came back, having
accomplished the mission, rejoicing![34]

The arms of Love

Thérèse teaches us to take Jesus literally and become
as children expecting everything from God. She saw all
her imperfections and inabilities clearly and honestly.
'I must bear with myself such as I am with all my
imperfections,' she said; she was always real, without
pretence, not tempted to imagine in some flight of
fantasy that she could follow the way of the great saints
because she saw clearly that she was, as we are, as
incapable as a child is to climb high, steep stairs
towards the healing, the fulfilment of heaven. So,
remaining a little child before God, she searched for '*a
little way, a way that is very straight, very short, and totally
new*':

> We are living now in an age of inventions, and
> we no longer have to take the trouble of climb-
> ing stairs, for, in the homes of the rich, an ele-
> vator has replaced these very successfully. I
> wanted to find an elevator which would raise
> me to Jesus, for I am too small to climb the
> rough stairway of perfection.[35]

She searched the inspiration of the Scriptures and
found these texts:

> Whoever is a *little one*, let him come to me.[36]

As one whom a mother caresses, so will I comfort you; you shall be carried at the breasts, and upon the knees they shall caress you.[37]

Thérèse has discovered her means to travel to heaven—that is, to live her life in Jesus and her eternity with God:

The elevator which must raise me to heaven is Your arms, O Jesus! And for this I had no need to grow up, but rather I had to remain *little and become this more and more.*[38]

We re-discover an old truth in the teaching of Jesus on the imperative of being as a little child, and that we must be spiritually born from above, born again. Thérèse in fact found her immediate inspiration and the proof of her teaching in the Old Testament texts given above. But Thérèse's sister, Céline, spoke of how Thérèse 'used to delight in pointing out to me various passages of the Gospel where there is reference to this spirit of childhood.'[39] In the teaching of the little way of love Thérèse has married the image of the little one clinging to Jesus with an image from modern times of the elevator which raises us. She teaches us that as little children we can place all our need and dependency on Jesus and travel in his arms.

We do not take ourselves to Jesus; we do not have the ability or strength to climb the steep stairs of salvation and perfection. Jesus sees our longing, and our goodwill in our continuing incompetent efforts, and he comes down to us to take us into his arms and carry us every single step. Thereby we go to healing, wholeness, holiness in the arms of Love by a new, direct, short way and we avoid the steep, hard slog up the stairway of holiness. The more we become weak and helpless and dependent, the more will he do for us in our blessed incompetence.

It was St Paul, who was trained in the school of the Pharisees but converted to the simple law of love, the great labourer who drove the Church and its new, saving message onto the arena of the whole world, who was converted to weakness and dependency on God, and wrote that 'it is not that we are so competent that we can claim any credit for ourselves; all our competence comes from God.'[40] Later, he extends the thought: 'For it is when I am weak that I am strong.'[41] Thérèse encapsulates the thought — 'It is Jesus who does everything in me; I do nothing except remain little and weak.' She echoes the words of the psalmist: 'I hold myself in quiet and silence, like a little child in its mother's arms, like a little child, so I keep myself.'[42]

> The little child expects everything from God
> as a child expects everything from its father.
> Knowing that it is weak and little,
> in humility the child seeks to become more and more so.
> The child is not discouraged over its faults,
> and is disquieted about nothing,
> for children fall often but are too little
> to hurt themselves very much.
> The child knows it is incapable of making its living,
> and can be raised to heaven only in Jesus' arms.

Chapter 3

Bold confidence in God's mercy and loving-kindness

Most of all I imitate the conduct of Magdalene; her
astonishing or rather her loving audacity which charms the
Heart of Jesus . . . even though I had on my conscience all the
sins that can be committed, I would go, my heart broken with
sorrow, and throw myself into Jesus' arms, for I know how
much He loves the prodigal child who returns to Him. . . . I
go to Him with confidence and love.

St Thérèse, *Story of a Soul*, XI, p. 258

Ovid, whose words on divine friendship we reflected
on in the introduction to this book, searched for his
god within the Roman pantheon of pagan gods. He did
not have the blessing of knowing about the God of the
Hebrews, nor of the advent of the Messiah among
them. In the year AD 8 he was sent from Rome into
exile for his remaining lifetime (some nine or ten years,
in the event) to the Black Sea on an uncomfortable,
unsettled frontier of the empire. In his emotional up-
heaval and distress he appealed for help from his wife
and friends. These entreaties are recorded in his poeti-
cal writings sent back to Rome from his banishment. In

them he comments that with the Augustan godhead appeased and made a friend, he cannot be downcast. Searching for divine mercy and loving-kindness, he appealed to a false god who failed him. He could never return to his beloved Rome.

Our history, the story of the human family, has been imbued with our religious experience. Our instinctive awareness of the unseen but ever-present has led us from the primitive fearful imagining of many gods veiled in the world around us on to the revealing of the one true God to his Chosen People, Israel. But even to them he remained One still frequently feared, appeased in complex ritualism. It required the visit of God himself, in his incarnation in Jesus, to complete the revelation of his truth as a God of mercy, the infinite fount of loving-kindness, one who is kind even to the ungrateful and the wicked.[1] But so often even to this day we read that God is Love and yet have so often not fully learned or been utterly confident in this fundamental truth. So, in considering Thérèse's teaching on bold confidence in God's mercy and loving-kindness, it would be helpful briefly to consider the circumstances of the earthly ministry of Jesus and the religious life of the Jewish people of that time; then, to look at some of our roots in earlier Christian experience and teaching showing the discovery and experience of the God of love.

In contrast to the heathen practices of their Roman contemporaries who enshrined many imagined gods, the Jewish people among whom Jesus grew up, taught and healed, remained faithful to the revelation to them of the one true God of Israel. But even they, in all their long pilgrimage throughout their troubled history, had not yet learned the full truth and they had deep divisions of opinion on the consequences of that search, leading to the existence of several schools of thought including those of the Pharisees and Sadducees.

The Pharisees studied the scriptures very closely and tried to apply their teaching to every aspect of daily life. This led sometimes to a legalistic, ritualistic observance which, in some cases, could overlook the exercise of a gentler, and indeed common-sense, love and mercy. This produced the tension between Jesus and some Pharisees often shown in the Gospels; as a group they have not enjoyed a good press among Christians. Meticulous and painstaking, such believers often served a strict and unrelenting God. Jesus told them that they had neglected justice and mercy while straining out gnats but swallowing camels.[2] Persons of this sort are, then, scrupulous in their religious observance. The word *scruple* — hence, scrupulous — is rooted in the Latin for a small, sharp stone, and such a stone in the conscience can hurt as much as a stone in the shoe. Frequently, we ourselves carry what we could perhaps call a Pharisaic part of us, not necessarily in the familiar sense of the accusation of hypocrisy, but in the sense that we find ourselves worried by painful scruples of conscience which deflect us from the real challenges and tasks before us. They are so often worries which do not get to the true heart of the matter, and they reduce our capacity to escape from formalistic compulsions into the freedom of love. St Paul was a Pharisee. After Jesus' death, it was his scrupulous, zealous search for, and persecution of, the new 'Jesus movement' which put him on the road which miraculously led to his conversion to Jesus. This leap from his own Pharisaic reading of the law to Christian love was a break for freedom, and he shares his rebirth with us in his insistence on the primacy of love, and on its gifts, in all his letters to the churches.

The Sadducees, the political manipulators seeking worldly advantage, were the other main party among the Jews at the time of Christ. They were the conservative 'establishment', including rich landowners, and the priesthood came mainly from them. They were wary of any threat to social peace from the more fervently religious Jews, even at the cost of adapting to the occupation by the pagan Romans of their holy land, a small and obscure province of the empire. Being conservative, they wanted stability. Their understanding of their religion was traditional and cautious of any innovation. They refused to accept the validity of any divine revelation after the Pentateuch (consisting of our Bible books of Genesis to Deuteronomy, traditionally ascribed to Moses) and rejected the development in later Jewish thought of belief in, for example, the immortality of the human soul and in angels.

The Jewish religious high council, the Sanhedrin, which condemned Jesus on charges of blasphemy for claiming to be the Son of God, the Christ[3] (meaning the Lord's Anointed, the Messiah) was composed of Sadducees and Pharisees in about equal numbers, given that the scribes, the prescribers of the many regulations based on the religious laws and traditions, allied themselves with the Pharisees. The Romans had removed the council's former power of the death penalty, therefore any case judged by it to merit death had to be referred to the Roman governor to obtain Roman condemnation and action.

While, then, the Pharisees and Sadducees settled for life under Roman occupation, many of Israel's children longed for freedom from pagan domination. Some clung to the vision of a Messiah of God bringing spiritual consummation; more dreamed of a great warrior liberator to lead them in defeating the Romans and establishing the kingship of God over a renewed, glorious Israel. This was seen by the Romans as an ever-present threat of political rebellion and chaos. No wonder, against the wider field of Jewish differences we have briefly reviewed, in his challenge to the established religious order of those days Jesus predicts his earthly end as one *counted as one of the rebellious.*[4] Indeed, when Jesus was charged before the Roman governor by the Sanhedrin, they were careful to translate their religious accusation into political terms which portrayed Jesus as an agitator, a would-be king inciting the people to revolt, to compel Pilate to condemn Jesus.[5] The Roman power had crucified rebel Jews before.

The little way of weakness and vulnerability

Against a background of much ritualistic ossification Jesus was a revolutionary—that is, he looked at things from the opposite point of view of so many people. To understand him, and he was frequently misunderstood, the world had to be turned upside down and the opposite way round. He was God but not obviously so. He did not come in the power and glory of the expected Messiah. Instead, his incarnation encapsulated the little way of weakness and vulnerability. He came in human form and spoke of the virtue of littleness. It was not until the Last Supper before his death that the disciples, in astonishment at his words, finally exclaimed that they now saw that Jesus knew everything and had indeed come from God.[6] But even then they yet had many things to learn, and would fail him before finally understanding. Then their failure was energized into a fertile following of Jesus throughout the known world.

Jesus revolutionized and reduced religion, if religious truth is understood (incorrectly) as being a great package of pious practices and complex compulsions. Beside the Ten Commandments, there are many other of God's guidelines laid down in the Mosaic writings. To these the Pharisees and scribes added their interpretations and rulings, leading to the many consequent detailed regulations to which they expected the people of Israel to conform. In opposition to their intricacy of rule and rote, Jesus stated that he had come to complete the law,[7] teaching a way of acting by which the goal of the law is to be fully realized. He tells us that we should be rooted in the two principal commandments of love.[8] From these two crucial commands flow all the fruitful consequences for which the Prophets under the old law had struggled with the Chosen People and so often suffered. In this radical reduction from ritualistic complexity and multiplicity we are set free,[9] and Jesus came to set us free so that we shall remain free.[10] From the slavery of the law, we are moved to Christ and to the freedom of the law of Love completed in him.

Released from anxiety and scrupulosity

From the compulsions laid on self in an anxiously scrupulous scouring of the soul, we are gifted to move outwards in the freedom of love. God gives love and acts in it, since he is Love. We respond in a free returning of that love which encompasses and emancipates our world. We are drawn from ourselves to him through his creation, we are released to freedom while remaining in the daily detail of our life here. We are called from self into community built by and on love. Then we can again see the fruitful loving God who creates us and walks with us in the garden in the cool of the day;[11] then we feel free to run eagerly to him rather than to fear him and elude the closeness of his embrace.

The two commandments of love are:

Love the Lord your God with all your heart, soul and mind;
and
love your neighbour as yourself. [12]
which Jesus underlined in his new command-

ment — 'you must love one another *just as I have loved you.*' [13]

From the fantasies and fiends of the pagans we move to the law which reveals the one true God; then on in the freedom of Jesus who reveals that we are called into close friendship with the God who is Love and Friendship.

Thérèse wrote, 'I do not understand souls who fear so tender a Friend. . . .' So aware did Thérèse become of the reality of the ever-present loving tenderness of God that she even questioned whether she would have more in heaven than she now had on earth, except that in heaven she would see the face of God. [14]

We now seek and serve God in the light of the teachings of Jesus, the Word of God faithfully revealed in the Church through the apostolic tradition and in the living words of its book the Bible.

Finding assurance in Scripture

In the Middle Ages the Latin Vulgate was the Church's official version of the Bible. But, in the turmoil of the Reformation amid a resurgence in the search for God and a desire for a more immediate experience of his love, there arose a demand for direct access by people generally to the Bible written in their everyday languages. Martin Luther (1483-1546) for example published his vernacular version having himself experienced a turmoil of questioning in the course of an austere life as an irreproachable monk and, later, priest. He achieved a doctorate in theology and became a professor of biblical studies, teaching Scripture at the University of Wittenberg. He lived very close to the words of Scripture.

Some years later he experienced a painful spiritual crisis — a storm of scruples. This inner questioning agitation apparently was caused by a theology on the action of God in his work of salvation which seemed to imply God's just but seemingly pitiless infliction of punishment on sinners. It was aggravated by the sight of the sale of indulgences. Luther was inundated by a sense of infinite unworthiness which could not be balanced with any number of good works or purchased acts of merit. Despite the conscientious regularity of his life, he felt in mortal danger. He searched the Scriptures in great agony of mind to find a way by which he could be peaceful in knowing a more certain assurance of the mercy of God. He made a discovery of loving-kindness. Years later he related this fundamental experience in his life:

> I felt that I was a sinner before God: my conscience was extremely disturbed, and I was by no means certain that God was appeased by my satisfactions. Moreover, I did not love this just and vengeful God. I hated Him, and if I did not blaspheme in secret, I was certainly indignant and murmured violently against Him. I said: 'Is it not enough that He condemns us to eternal death because of the sin of our fathers, and that He makes us undergo all the severity of the law?. . .' Finally God

took pity on me. While I was meditating, day
and night, and examining the implications of
the words 'The righteousness of God is revealed in the gospel, as it is written: the righ-
teous shall live by faith,' I began to
understand . . . God in His mercy justifies us
by means of faith . . . Immediately I felt myself reborn, and I seemed to have entered the
broad gates of Paradise itself. . . .[15]

Born again, Luther found the merciful peace he
needed and the assurance that we are not saved as from
our own efforts and struggles but by faith, by living
belief in God's freely given grace; an unearned,
unmerited, gratuitous and strengthening gift. St Paul
had written: 'For all who believe in Jesus, no distinction
is made — all have sinned and all are justified, infused
with God's grace as a free gift, being set free in Jesus';[16]
and so, 'justified by a living faith, are at peace with God
through Jesus,[17] living under grace to be instruments of
uprightness.'[18] In a living faith, we are regenerated,
reborn from above, called to love.

Luther had no intention of splitting the then
undivided Church in the West. He merely wished to
reform it; the Church composed of sinners is always in
need of reform and renewal. However, in the complex
of later events the catastrophe of division took place
and Christian brothers and sisters moved apart, each
further to explore the rich experience of finding God,
but unable to share their experiences across the divide
in the encampment of Christ. Thankfully, we are now

moving into the ability to listen to each other, to enable Jesus to heal his followers in unity beneath his one banner.

Luther, like Thérèse, broke with the idea of any pedantic spiritual accountancy, the acquisitive amassing of merit through good works. Luther summed up his view very simply: good works do not make a good person but a good person does good works. Thérèse wrote: 'I understand so well that it is only love which makes us acceptable to God that this love is the only good I ambition . . . Jesus does not demand great actions from us but simply surrender [that is, trusting confidence in him] and gratitude [that is, reciprocating love].'[19] On another occasion, told that a certain event had been a source of *merits* for her, she replied, 'Not *merits*! . . . If I had amassed *merits*, I would have despaired immediately.'[20] She, like Luther, based her spiritual optimism upon the good news of the Scriptures. 'How blessed are those to whom God attributes uprightness, apart from any action taken, to whom the Lord imputes no guilt.'[21]

The ending of spiritual accountancy

Thérèse, like Luther, moved far from the self-justifying spirituality which was round her. In our compulsive activity, it is something of a shock to hear Thérèse reflect upon her relegation, during her final illness, to inability to carry out her normal duties (which among other things included four or five hours each day praying and singing the Divine Office) unconcerned that others of the community might think her a useless member: 'As far as that is concerned, it is the least of my worries; it makes no difference to me at all'.[22] A little earlier she had said:

> It is impossible, I know, but if God were not to see my good actions, I would not be the least bit disturbed by it. I love Him so much that I'd like to please Him without His being aware of it. When He knows it and sees it, He is obliged to reward me, and I don't want Him to have to go to this trouble.[23]

We go to God by simply answering his call in a loving response of mind and heart, freed from any worry about 'earning' his joy in us. This is emphasized by Thérèse when she said to someone made very sad by their apparent lack of works: 'Even if I had accomplished all the works of St Paul, I would still believe myself to be a *useless servant*.[24] But it is precisely this that makes up my joy, for having nothing, I shall receive everything from God.'[25]

Jesus loved beyond all others

Even before Luther, in the latter half of the fifteenth century, there was a remarkable spiritual renewal in a movement called the *Devotio Moderna* — which can be translated as 'the modern devotion to serving God' — to assist in providing for a wave of religious interest and longing among 'ordinary' people. Among those immersed in this renewal was Thomas à Kempis

(1379-?), who wrote *The Imitation of Christ*, after the Bible one of the widest read of books, refreshing and reinvigorating to this day. Thérèse placed her first and final reliance on the Scriptures but also prized the *Imitation* as a wellspring of inspiration and confirmation over the years while she was receiving her ideas on the little way. This excerpt on close friendship with Jesus relates to our discussion and gives a flavour of the warm Jesus-centred, love-based spirituality which has touched the lives of millions:

> You cannot live happily without a friend—and if Jesus is not your friend beyond all others, you will find yourself very sad and lonely. . . . Of all you hold dear, let Jesus only be your especial love.
>
> You must love all people for the sake of Jesus, but you must love Jesus for himself; and Jesus Christ is the only person who may be loved beyond all others, for he alone is good and faithful, beyond all other friends.[26]

We cannot of ourselves earn this friendship, but we are invited by Jesus freely to ask for it.[27]

The confident seeking of an intimate, warm friendship with Jesus goes back through the centuries. We can feel especially attached to an English saint of the fourteenth century, Mother Julian of Norwich. Her age was very troubled. The outbreak of the Black Death plague in 1348-1350 was similar in effect to that of a major nuclear disaster. Some one third of the population of Europe perished. Over the remaining years of that century the dreaded scourge periodically returned. Out of this distress, Julian raises a voice of optimism, good humour and even joy. She explains that in 1373 she herself, at the age of thirty-one years, had been sick almost to the point of death and had prepared herself for it. She was extremely sad to die so young since she wished to live so that here she could know and love God more deeply, and so prize him more dearly when finally in heaven. She had no fear of his mercy, trusting him completely. The response by God was to give her a number of visions of Jesus' Passion. Julian recovered and spent the next twenty years prayerfully thinking out the meaning of these visions, receiving 'inward teaching' to help her understand. She wrote her account of this seeking and finding, which has been rediscovered in this century. These are some relevant extracts from the *Revelations of Divine Love:*

> It seems to me that the greatest joy we shall ever know comes from seeing the wonderful kindness and friendship of our Father who is our Creator, in our Lord Jesus Christ, who is our Brother and our Saviour.
>
> For the ground of mercy is love, and it is mercy's task to keep us safe in love. This was revealed to me in such a way that when I looked I could not separate mercy from love. Mercy is a sweet, gracious, loving activity, full of pity. Mercy is at work within us, protecting

us, and making sure that everything turns out to the best for us. . . . I was forced to agree that it is our anger that is calmed and dispelled by the mercy and forgiveness of God.

So Jesus is our true Mother in nature because of our first creation, and He is our true Mother in grace because He took our created nature. In the Second Person [Jesus] there is all the loving service and sweet spontaneous care that belongs to beloved motherhood . . .[28]

Julian comments that this revelation to her does not itself make her good. She is only good if as a result she loves God better. 'I know for certain that there are many who have not had any revelations or visions outside the ordinary teaching of Holy Church and yet love God better than I do,' she added. She speaks for, and to, 'ordinary' people like us, because she did not seek to depart from the ordinary ways of devotion: 'I was not seeking a physical vision or revelation of God, but the natural compassion of a soul for our Lord Jesus Christ.'

Common sense speaks to our common condition

Julian was full of that common sense which speaks immediately to our common condition. She valued the plain, unvisioned way by which most of us have to travel in ordinary faith. Her spirit is akin to that of Thérèse, since neither viewed personal visions nor such special experiences as essential or intrinsically desirable. God dispenses his gifts as and how he wills, providing for each all that is needed and most suited to each on the way to full friendship with him. Like little children, in a comment made by Thérèse, we shut our eyes and trustingly open our hands to receive what God wishes to give us.

Thérèse, following a plain unvisioned way, one of plain bold confidence, teaches that we are not to be afraid of God, but be open and honest with him as a Friend. We should not stand afar and feel unworthy and fearful, but go close to him and boldly have confidence in him. After looking at a picture representing Jesus with two little children, the *smaller* one having climbed onto his lap, the other remaining at his feet, kissing his hand, Thérèse commented that she was the smaller one who has climbed onto his lap without fear, the other one is acting like an adult who has been told something and knows that he must have respect for Jesus![29] Another time, she reproved her sister for not carrying out her teaching to be familiar with the figure of Jesus on the crucifix—not simply to kiss Jesus on the feet but to go closer and to kiss him on the face on both cheeks.[30] Thérèse listened to the Gospel and took Jesus at his word, for he had invited a bold, familiar approach (that is, as a close family member) replete with importunity and insistence: 'I'll torment God so much that, if He wanted to refuse me at first, my importunity will force Him to grant my desires. This story [31] is in the Gospel.'[32] God surely wishes us to be real: he is working in us, if we allow it (for always he respects our freedom) to real-ize us as he uniquely made each of us, for himself as his children of love. There could be no other purpose since he is Love; in love there is no room for fear for love casts out *all* fear,[33] every last vestige of it until love is cast into Love. Thérèse commented to her Prioress on being open to God within the particular way, envisioned or unvisioned, by which he calls and leads each one:

How different are the variety of ways through which the Lord leads souls! In the lives of the saints, we find many of them who didn't want to leave anything of themselves behind after their death, not the smallest souvenir, not the least bit of writing. On the contrary, there are others, like our holy Mother St Teresa [of Avila] who have enriched the Church with their lofty revelations, *having no fears of revealing the secrets of the King*[34] in order that they can make Him more loved and known by souls. Which of these two types of saints is more pleasing to God? It seems to me they are equally pleasing to Him, since all of them followed the inspiration of the Holy Spirit. . . . Yes, all is well when one seeks only the will of Jesus.[35]

Love longs and thirsts for each and everyone

We are, then, graced by an ever longing Love which thirsts for each and every one of us. In it we can confidently enjoy the glorious freedom of the children of God[36] having the first-fruits of the Spirit which is Love,[37] whose call to us totally frees us from need of that fear and hesitancy—that mistaken, false humility which is the product of self-doubt and lack of confidence—which we have too often and mistakenly derived from our belief. We can be boldly confident in that love, and in the longing, thirsting Father of mercy and loving-kindness. 'Pity, born of love, protects us in our times of need, and longing, born from that same love, draws us up to Heaven. God thirsts for mankind to come to Him . . . and still he continues to thirst and long,' as Mother Julian wrote from her visions.[38]

Julian understood from the teachings of her visions that if I pay attention to myself alone, I am nothing at all—but within the Body of Christ (that is, the *family* of the Church) I am united to all in love, depending for my life on this unity in Jesus. In this oneness of the family of Jesus there are members with different gifts, and the gifts are given to serve others in and by the love of God.[39] Teresa of Avila gave thanks that she was a daughter of the Church founded on earth by Jesus to be the guardian of the truth. Similarly, Thérèse saw vocations and fruitfulness as the gifts which are only fully realized within community. Such gifts are the exchange of love within the creativity of God. Thérèse searched for a more clear and profound understanding of her vocation within the Body of Christ, the *community* of the Church:

I opened the Epistles of St Paul . . . Chapters 12 and 13 of the First Epistle to the Corinthi-

ans fell under my eyes. I read there, in the first
of these chapters, that all cannot be apostles,
prophets, doctors, etc., that the Church is
composed of different members, and that the
eye cannot be the hand at one and the same
time. . . . I continued my reading, and this
sentence consoled me: 'Yet strive after the
better gifts, and I point out to you a yet more
excellent way.'[40] And the Apostle explains
how all the most perfect gifts are nothing
without love. That charity is the excellent
way that leads most surely to God . . . Considering the mystical body of the Church, I
had not recognized myself in any of the members described by St Paul, or rather I desired
to see myself in them all. *Charity* gave me the
key to my vocation. I understood that if the
Church had a body composed of different
members, the most necessary and most noble
of all could not be lacking to it, and so I understood that the Church had a Heart and
that this Heart was burning with love. I understood that it was Love alone that made the
Church's members act, that if Love ever became extinct, apostles would not preach the
Gospel and martyrs would not shed their
blood. I understood that Love comprised all
vocations, that Love was everything, that it
embraced all times and places . . . in a word,
that it was eternal! . . . Yes, I have found my
place in the Church and it is You, O my God,

who have given me this place; in the heart of
the Church, my Mother, I shall be Love. Thus
I shall be everything. . . .[41]

In her writing about her final discovery of her
vocation we should notice that Thérèse uses the initial
capital letter when referring to Love. Her fearless,
unrestrained offering of herself causes her to offer not
just to be loving, or love, but *be Love*, the very essence of
God. She will be everything. This level of intemperate
importunity and insistence, this bold confidence, was
invited by Jesus.[42] We remember that Thérèse herself
said that she did nothing that could not be done by any
little child of God, knowing that the lower a soul the
more God would stoop to it with delight. The gifts
which God bears to us are unlimited, if we accept his
loving invitation with bold confidence, *never* in *any*
circumstance fearing him.

Called by vocation out of ourselves

We can consider certain implications of the search
for vocation, as in Thérèse's search for her own
vocation. The word *vocation* is rooted in the Latin for *to
call*. In itself the act of calling is towards an other. We
do not call to ourselves. We are called to our vocation.

We are called out of the enclosure of self by Jesus, to
him, within the web of relationships of his creation. It
is like moving from death into life; Jesus called,
'Lazarus, come out!' and the dead man came out, still
bound hand and foot with a cloth over his face. It is

important to note that next Jesus told those round him, *'Unbind him, let him go free.'*[43] Jesus immediately involves those round us in his action. We have to first respond; then it is in our movement into community, perhaps at first disbelieving and hesitant, our movement into the web of relationships between all others that we make real the call of Jesus and realize our freedom.

The Christian belief in the Holy Trinity is a revelation of the *community* of the Godhead which said, 'Let *us* make man in *our* own image, in the likeness of *ourselves.'*[44] To exist, as the human beings we are, is to be dependent in relationships with other beings. As Julian said, if I pay attention to myself alone, I am nothing at all. Our life depends upon sharing, unity, community — in its dependence upon the Godhead of the Holy Trinity, in the likeness of which we are made. Outside loving, supportive community we become isolated and lonely; to centre upon myself is painful because this isolates me and deprives me even further.

The drive of our society is towards the satisfaction of each in our needs; in itself this is very laudable in the face of so much poverty and suffering in the past. But this drift also generates that individualism which emphasizes self-satisfaction. The balance is changing and appears to be eroding our sense of deep inter-dependency and the relationships we need to realize ourselves. I now can make autonomous decisions based upon my own perceived needs considered in themselves — I am told that I am free and able to act on self-determination, which in the event seems some form of self-isolation. The situation concerning abortion is a case in point. Our law enables an autonomous decision by the person concerning her own body. The full relationship, with new dependent life, is easily overlooked. The weaker one is put at discount to the stronger one. This is contrary to the law of love, which upholds the weak. Self-satisfaction conveniently overlooks the community of life and ultimately is self-defeating. Our true need and welfare is in community, interdependency, in *all* its aspects. It is clear that all our modern State reforms and provisions and dependency do not supply this need.

Mother Teresa of Calcutta visited Cuba and spoke to Fidel Castro, the President, and raised with him the needs of the poor. Castro explained that the State now provided the people with what they needed. 'It cannot give love,' Mother Teresa replied.

Called by Love into Love

Jesus' call is always to love, and our vocation is always realized in love. Love is relationship. In isolation, closed in on myself, I cannot love myself, I only find a hate for self, because I am not related as God intended. When he made us he made us from his community, and he said, 'It is not right that the man should be alone'[45] and so he gave us helpers. We are the creatures of community, made by the divine community, the one indivisible Trinity. In community we must love our neighbour as ourselves because we do not find our true selves without our neighbour. We cannot truly love ourselves as God intended, within the flow of his love, until we find ourselves through our neighbour in community. 'No one who fails to love the brother whom he can see can love God whom he has not seen.'[46]

Jesus our Friend calls each of us out to him; he gifts each with a task, a calling, a vocation. Our calling, our vocation is rooted in the Love which is God. As Julian said, in the Body of Christ we are united in love and the life of all of us depends on that unity which is Jesus the Christ.

The release from perplexity in ourselves is surely in the release of self towards others in Jesus. Then we are able to share the perplexity of others and accompany Jesus as he releases them. Surely our calling from Jesus and our vocation gifted by him is in love—to be Love; '. . . I am alive; yet it is no longer I, but Christ living in me,' as St Paul expressed it.[47]

Thérèse was reflecting on the mystery of the different ways in which Jesus calls souls to him. She wondered at the way in which some are called to spiritual greatness which is apparent in this world—for example, St Paul and St Teresa of Avila among many others—and why the same such grace is not apparently given to everyone:

> I wondered why poor savages died in great numbers without even having heard the Name of God pronounced. Jesus deigned to teach me this mystery. He set before me the book of nature; I understood how all the flowers he has created are beautiful, how the splendour of the rose and the whiteness of the

lily do not take away the perfume of the little
violet or the delightful simplicity of the daisy.
I understood that if all flowers wanted to be
roses, nature would lose her springtime
beauty, and the fields would no longer be
decked out with little wild flowers.

And so it is with the world of souls, Jesus'
garden . . .

I understood, too, that Our Lord's love is revealed as perfectly in the most simple soul that
resists His grace in nothing as in the most excellent soul; in fact, since the nature of love is
to humble oneself, if all souls resembled those
of the holy Doctors who illumined the Church
with the clarity of their teachings, it seems
God would not descend so low when coming
to their heart. But He created the child who
knows only how to make his feeble cries heard;
He has created the poor savage who has nothing but the natural law to guide him. It is to
their hearts that God deigns to lower Himself.
These are the wild flowers whose simplicity attracts Him. When coming down in this way,
God manifests His infinite grandeur . . . everything works out for the good of each soul.[48]

All are called

Thérèse is considering the action of divine grace not
only in, as it were, its amount for any individual—and

the conclusion must be that each soul is offered fulfilment to its own unique and complete bliss at the pleasure of God — but she is also reflecting the universality of Jesus' salvific action throughout his human creation. His call also can be heard in the hearts of those who have not had the blessing of hearing his Name through their ears. This understanding of the universality of the call of God is in the statement of the Second Vatican Council held in the early 1960's:

> Those who, *through no fault of their own,* do not know the Gospel of Christ or his Church, but who nevertheless seek God with a sincere heart, and, moved by grace, try in their actions to do his will as they know it through the dictates of their conscience — these too may achieve salvation. Nor shall divine providence deny the assistance necessary for salvation to those who, *without any fault of theirs,* have not arrived at an explicit knowledge of God, and who, not without grace, strive to lead a good life. Whatever good or truth is found among them is considered by the Church to be a preparation for the Gospel and given by him who enlightens *all* men that they may at length have life.[49]

Thérèse centred herself upon Jesus, and upon his incarnation, the taking upon himself of that human flesh and form he had created for us. Her full name in the convent was Thérèse of the Child Jesus and of the

Holy Face, and her choice reflects her insights into the spiritual significance of littleness and dependency, and her acute perception of the totality of divine Love which gives without limit, even to the dire extremity of the freely-chosen cross; and without requirement of that complexity which so many Christians have mistakenly associated with the response to God's love. Jesus himself, as we have seen, 'reduced' the law to the two greatest commands which encompass all God's commands. Understanding our utter weakness, he lightened our load to enable us to travel to him. 'Come to me, all you who labour and are overburdened, and I will give you rest . . . you will find rest for your souls. Yes, my yoke is easy and my burden light.'[50] Jesus spoke thus to break the hard impositions which were laid upon the children of Israel through the inflexible interpretation of the law by the religious 'establishment' of his day. But Jesus was steeped in the Scriptures and he still remembered the many promises made by an ever kindly God—Level up, level up, clear the way, remove the obstacles from my people's way . . . 'I live in the holy heights but I am with the contrite and humble, to revive the spirit of the humble, to revive the heart of the contrite. . . . I saw how he behaved, but I shall heal him, I shall lead him, fill him with consolation.'[51]

Thérèse also knew Scripture and understood the need to reassure others and encourage them, confident that amid the rather duty-strewn religion of her contemporaries she could teach of a kindlier God. Her teaching immediately reminds us of the gentle understandings of Mother Julian in her references to the Divine Motherhood:

> I assure you that God is even kinder than you think. He is satisfied with a look, a sigh of love . . . I have realized that all one has to do is to take *Jesus by the heart*. Consider a small child who has displeased his mother, by flying into a rage or perhaps disobeying her; if he sulks in a corner and screams in fear of punishment, his mother will certainly not forgive his fault; but if he comes to her with his little arms out-stretched, smiling and saying: 'Kiss me, I won't do it again,' surely his mother will im-mediately press him tenderly to her heart, for-getting all that he has done.[52]

To a distressed person who had written about his desire to repent and change, who would now *drag* himself to the feet of Jesus to ask pardon for all previous offences, Thérèse wrote this, to encourage him instead to simply cast himself into Jesus' arms:

> He has long forgotten your infidelities, only your desires for perfection are present to give joy to His heart . . . For those who love Him and, after each discourteous act, cast them-selves into His arms and ask pardon, Jesus is vibrant with joy. He says to His angels what the prodigal son's father said to his servants: 'Put on him the first robe, put a ring on his

hand, and let us make merry,' How little are Jesus' *kindness* and *merciful love* realized! It is true that, to enjoy His riches, we must humble ourselves, see our own nothingness, which is what many souls will not do; but you do not act like them, so the way of simple loving confidence is indeed the way for you. I would have you be *simple* with the good God . . .[53]

Disquieted and discouraged by nothing

For those who love him . . . that is the only condition. Thérèse teaches that those who love him are not to become discouraged and full of baseless scruples even when in failure amid temptations:

> We must disregard all these temptations, pay no attention to them. The devil must indeed be clever to deceive a soul like that! But surely you know that that is the one goal of his desires. He realizes, treacherous creature that he is, that he cannot get a soul to sin when that soul wants to belong wholly to Jesus, so he only tries to make it *think* that it is in sin.[54]

We are to be disquieted about nothing and are not to be discouraged over faults and failings, Thérèse stresses, giving her own confidence amid imperfections as a model for us, and further teaching that the involuntary faults of those who love Him do not pain God, for children fall often but are too small to hurt themselves very much.[55] Jesus would not inspire the longings to please him without facilitating fruition. Thérèse expressed her tranquil confidence in God's limitless love saying that she had heard Jesus' words to the prodigal son, his words to Mary Magdalen, to the woman caught in adultery, and to the Samaritan woman; nobody could frighten her because she knew what to believe concerning his love and mercy. 'Even though I had on my conscience all the sins that can be committed, I would go, my heart broken with sorrow, and throw myself into Jesus' arms . . . I go to Him with confidence and love.'[56]

The little child knows that God
is more tender than any mother.
Love penetrates and surrounds the child
in the eternal embrace of merciful loving-kindness.
The child knows that the faults of his child
do not cause God any pain;
love will quickly consume everything,
leaving only a profound peace and joy of heart.
In Jesus' arms, never discouraged,
the child is launched on waves of love and bold confidence.

Chapter 4

Tranquil trust in the actions of God's limitless love

My director, Jesus, does not teach me to count my acts, but to do everything for love, to refuse Him nothing, to be pleased when He gives me a chance to prove to Him that I love Him — but all this in peace, in abandonment; Jesus does everything, I nothing.

St Thérèse, *Letter to Céline,* 6 July 1893

The way to committed, trusting faith in a living, loving God in any individual life may indeed have to come first as a way of disturbance, of an overturning, of a disorientation before a new peaceful re-alignment. Of its premise and nature, the course of a life of faith is unknown ahead of its unfolding events; faith and trust are essentially exercised in blindness. 'I shall lead the blind by a road they do not know, by paths they do not know I shall conduct them.'[1]

If a chapter on having tranquil trust in the actions of Jesus seems surprisingly to begin by discussing unsettlement, perhaps we should remind ourselves of the experiences of the Hebrew people, particularly during the dramatic happening only three months into their long trek through the desert from Egypt to the land promised by God — the land of milk and honey, the land of repose after journey and struggle in the desert. The people were still rebellious, looking back to the seeming security and the provisions of their captivity in fertile Egypt and unsettled in the discomforts of their desert journey amid scarcity. They were not yet prepared for full commitment to, and complete trust in, the God who would lead them to a new but unknown life.

As Moses and the entire Chosen People were being prepared for their long pilgrimage and a final commitment to the one true God and to his covenant with them, the scene was awesome. The Bible provides a graphic picture. As a cloud of deep darkness covered the holy mountain from which would issue the call and commandments of God, thunder and lightning erupted amid great sounds pealing round the gathered people like a blasting of trumpet. This was the day when the world was to be remade through the revelations of God and of his way. The people were stricken with terror, they kept their wary distance. In their dismay they trembled, imploring their leader Moses: 'Do not let God speak to us, or we shall die.'[2]

'My face,' said God, 'you cannot see for no human being can see me and survive.'[3]

Moses approached Yahweh God on the mountain to ask him to show his way for a committed people. The Lord Yahweh, *He Who Is,* maker and master of all that is seen and unseen, all that is past and all that is to come, replied: 'I myself shall go with you and I shall give you rest . . . I shall do what you have asked, because you enjoy my favour and because I know you by name.'[4] Approaching close to God at his invitation, Moses, for all the people, found not the God they had feared but the God of limitless love!

Moreover, Scripture tells us that Yahweh God talked with Moses face to face as one talks to a friend.[5] He is a Friend who knows his friend by name, who gives his friend favour and rest, who travels with his friend and does as his friend asks.

When we discover and come to Yahweh God, we approach the one who is indescribably All and we are prepared as were the Chosen People, because we too are now chosen. First, we too must be stripped and washed, and then be sanctified[6] — first hollowed and then hallowed. We ourselves cannot do this, for we too are trembling; we are incapable and he must do it for us. So he says *to* us and *of* us:

> This is why I shall block her way with thorns . . .
> and lead her out into the desert
> and speak to her heart . . .
> and make the Vale of Misfortune into a gateway
>   of hope.[7]

Then in our disturbance we find not the God we had feared but the God of love who says: *He knows each of us by name. We enjoy his favour. He will go with us and give us rest. He will do as we ask. He will make our valley of misfortune into a gateway of hope.*

For now, thus says Yahweh,

Do not be afraid for I have redeemed you;
I have called you by your name, you are mine.
Should you pass through the waters, I shall be
    with you;
or through rivers, they will not swallow you
    up.
Should you walk through fire, you will not
    suffer,
and the flame will not burn you.
For I am Yahweh, your God,
the Holy One of Israel, your Saviour.[8]

There she will respond to me as when she was
    young,
as on the day she came up from Egypt.
When that day comes—declares Yahweh—
you will call me 'my husband.'
I will betroth you to myself for ever
I will betroth you in uprightness and justice,
and faithful love and tenderness.
Yes, I shall betroth you to myself in loyalty
and in the knowledge of Yahweh.[9]

Fools in Christ

But it is essential to note that prior to that, he had told the Chosen People that before their release into the desert, guided by him for the remainder of their journey to the Promised Land, they must for seven days eat unleavened bread; flat, dense bread without yeast,[10] which is hard to bite upon and chew. 'I shall block her way with thorns, and lead her out into the desert.'

There are those whom life has prepared in a hard way before they are washed and quickened. They have not avoided perplexity and misfortune, but have lived with it and accepted it and have learned from it. They are blessed because they have accepted and eaten their hard unleavened bread. Their way has already been blocked with thorns. Then the way seems a very quick, peaceful way.

At the Home for the Dying which Mother Teresa established in Calcutta:

> there was a man who had cancer, his body half-consumed by the sickness. Everyone had abandoned him as a hopeless case. Mother Teresa came near him to wash him tenderly. She encountered, at first, only the sick man's disdain.
>
> 'How can you stand my body's stench?' he asked.
>
> Then, quite calmly, the dying man said to her, 'You're not from here. The people here don't behave the way you do.'
>
> Several minutes went by. Then the terminally ill man murmured a typical Indian expression: 'Glory to you, woman.'
>
> 'No,' replied Mother Teresa, 'Glory to you who suffer with Christ.'

Then they smiled at each other. The sick
man's suffering seemed to stop. He died two
days later.[11]

Surely this was tranquil trust in the actions of God's
love — and it was in a man who had nothing else. He
was poor in body and he was poor in spirit. Of such,
Jesus tells us, is made the kingdom of God.[12] As Paul
said, they are fools, in Christ.[13] Faith is accepted
quietly, peacefully by those who do not have a false
pride, having been prepared and stripped by life
already. Their way has already been blocked by thorns;
they have been prepared and have eaten their
unleavened bread.

Such people may not necessarily be poor in worldly
goods, but nevertheless they are truly poor in
spirit — like Joseph of Arimathaea who on the *day of
preparation* claimed Jesus and shared his tomb with
him, and longed for the kingdom of heaven.[14] Or, like
St Thomas More, rising to become the high Lord
Chancellor of the realm, next to the King himself and
yet poor in spirit; prepared, he said, to eat the bread of
poverty or of plenty entirely as the Lord chose to
provide. Or like St Margaret Clitherow of York during
her life as the wife of a prosperous merchant, but
nevertheless whose 'most desire,' she said, 'was to eat
rye bread,' the bread of the poor, and who emptied the
chamber pots of the house herself, prepared to do this
distasteful task herself rather than have her servants
perform it.

God permits you to be forgotten

In a contrasting incident, Sister Marie of the Trinity tells us of her correction by Thérèse:

> they forgot to serve me with dessert at dinner. Afterwards I went to the infirmary to see Sister Thérèse and found the sister who sits next to me in the refectory there before me. I skilfully let her know that I had been forgotten. Sister Thérèse heard me and made me go and bring it to the notice of the sister who serves the desserts. I implored her not to make me do this, but she said, 'No, that's your penance; you're not worthy of the sacrifice God asks of you. He asked you to do without dessert, because it was He who permitted you to be forgotten. He thought you were generous enough to make this sacrifice, and you disappointed Him by drawing attention to the fact.' Her lesson bore fruit and cured me entirely.[15]

On another occasion Thérèse said to Marie: 'Jesus loves people who are cheerful and ready to smile. So, when are you going to be able to hide your sufferings from Him and to sing to Him that you are prepared to suffer with Him?'[16]

If we are not prepared, if in fear of the new and unknown we cling to the false security and sour provisions of our captivity in Egypt, the fundamental commitment of faith may come as a thief by night, taking by surprise and stripping ill-gotten possessions, our false certainty, our self-pride. Such faith is gained in disturbing rebirth, because we have not waited prepared and ready to open the door as soon as he knocks.[17]

The baby entering the struggle of birth is certainly disturbed and inconvenienced, and the event brings it naked to a world of change and challenge, of light and cold and heat, very different from the enclosing, darkened security of the womb. From that security the child moves, amid its first cries, into that reality in which it will have to find faith—faith in those who care and provide for it in its incapability. Faith is a facing of reality, a way to be open, vulnerable to a God who may if necessary seem one of surprises and inconveniences, a God of unknowing.

Living faith then comes like a wounding, a healing wound which reveals through its edges what is in us and that which we, if not prepared, may have forgotten in our distraction to lesser things. As Thérèse noted:

> He has struck us a great blow, but a blow of Love . . . God is admirable, but above all He is loveable, so let us love Him.[18]

As the Old Testament prophet says, 'From dawn to dark you have been making an end of me; till daybreak, I cried for help; like a lion, he has crushed all my bones, from dawn to dark you have been making an end of me.'[19]

A God of jealousy and real intent

What has happened to this 'gentle Jesus, meek and mild' of Charles Wesley's hymn? What has happened to the toned-down, time-patinated figure of popular imagination — reduced to one comfortably possessed, with whom we may spend some comforting time periodically? He has suddenly become a disturber, a threat.

He is as a burglar coming in the shadows of the night.[20] He is a master who arrives unheralded and causes weeping and grinding of teeth.[21] He is the flashing lightning, striking East and West.[22] He is one of whom we are warned to be on the alert.[23]

The imagery may make us wonder: has the belief in a God of kindliness misled us? With the psalmist, we can puzzle. . . . Will he for ever reject and no more show his favour, has his love vanished, his promise come to an end . . . has he forgotten his compassion and his mercy, shutting off his tenderness in anger?[24]

He is a God of jealousy[25] and real intent. The longing of this Spirit sent to make his home in us is a jealous longing, brooking no accommodation with the world as a competitor, giving his favour only to the humble.[26] His intention, and the infinite dimension and strength of that intention, was shown in Calvary. He has bought us and paid for us. In his intent, he has a way of breaking in on our games. If necessary, he is prepared to let us break ourselves, be reduced, noughted, so that he may do the re-building, so that he is the foundation stone and the cornerstone and the capping stone. 'I have come to bring fire to the earth and how I wish it were blazing already!'[27] *Here is the teacher that I am giving you; he will teach you everything that you must do.*[28] Then I am driven, from the ruins made by my own work, to call out: Lord, I am overwhelmed, come to my help![29] I am caught in my folly; but my folly is nothing compared to the folly of God who loves me to the point of distraction from his peace and bliss from all eternity, as Thérèse points out:

> One judges others by oneself, and as the world is stupid it naturally thinks that we are the stupid ones! But after all, we are not the first. The one crime charged against Jesus by Herod was that He was mad . . . and I agree with him! Yes, it was folly to seek the poor little hearts of mortals to make them His thrones, He, the King of Glory, Who is throned above the Cherubim! He Whose presence is mightier than the Heavens can contain! Our Beloved was mad to come down to earth seeking sinners to make them His friends, His intimates, to make them like unto Himself, when He was perfectly happy with the two adorable Persons of the Trinity! We shall never be able to commit the follies for Him that He has committed for us, nor do our actions deserve the name of folly, for they are in fact most reasonable acts, far below what our love would like to accomplish. So it is the world which is stupid, not realizing what Jesus has done to save it.[30]

Then as I cry out in my need and folly, Jesus cures me and restores me to life; my bitterness turns to well-being, for he preserves me from the pit of destruction and thrusts all my sins behind him.[31] I am less than nothingness, and what I do is less than nothing;[32] but what is done is the awesome work of the Lord who alone works such wonders.[33] Then my happiness is being in Jesus my refuge, and it is his work alone of which I tell with wonder.[34] For Charles Wesley was wise; the second line of his hymn is: 'Look upon a little child.' Jesus is gentle with children.

Merit does not consist in doing or giving much

As Thérèse taught, Jesus does everything, I do nothing; and he does not inflict but simply comes to claim his own, that which he made and named:

Merit does not consist in doing or giving much, but in receiving, in loving much. It is said that 'it is more blessed to give than to receive'[35] and that is true; but when Jesus wants to make His own the blessedness of giving, it would not be gracious to refuse. Let Him take and give what He chooses, perfection consists of doing His will; and the soul which gives itself totally to Him is called by Jesus 'His mother, His sister,' and His whole family.[36] And more than that: 'If anyone loves me, he will keep my word [which means he will do my will] and my Father will love him

and we will come to him and make our abode
with him.'[37] . . . All one has to do is to love
Him, not considering oneself, not examining
one's faults too closely.[38]

We can hardly have a comprehensive trust in the
actions of God's love until we have a comprehensive
disbelief in our own incapable, unaided actions.

Jesus' words on the *necessity* of being born from above,
being born again, perhaps reflect the fact that if our belief
was given to us in our childhood, something with which
we have grown up and accepted as a feature of our life,
part of the given scenery we have taken for granted, then
our childish understanding may now need to face the real
challenge of real faith, which disturbs and turns things
upside down and changes us fundamentally so that the
world is never the same again. Or we may be coming to
faith in Jesus from a life of rebellion from which we have
many habits of thought, ways and assumptions which are
impediments to the flow of grace in us. We will not
always be aware of these and our attention needs to be
drawn to them, for they must be reduced and noughted
in order that our new life can flourish and be fruitful, for
our own sakes, and for those others for whom we are
intended in turn to be gospels of good news. If one has
not experienced the disturbance of self, then maybe one
ought to look carefully to ensure it is not needed. We
have many clever and convenient ways to avoid the
inconvenient.

Our God is inconvenient, and so we may have
self-accommodatingly resorted to a false image of him,

re-making him to a being comfortably reflecting our own desires and being, our very own creature of our own convenience; comfortably lived with while we say 'Lord, Lord. . .'[39] It was the son who refused to go and then went, and not the son who said he would go and didn't, who did the Father's will, in the company of prostitutes and tax collectors.[40]

God loves us infinitely, past human comprehension and past any telling of words. In our incompleteness we can only catch a shadow of the thirst, the longing he has for us; and ever in this world it remains a complete mystery. So we are driven in the end to trust what we do not understand; as Thérèse says:

> One must consent to stay always poor and without strength, and that's the difficulty, for where are we to find the man truly poor in spirit? He must be sought afar, says the psalmist. He does not say we must look for Him among great souls, but 'afar,' that is in *lowliness, nothingness.* Let us stay *very far* from all that is brilliant, let us love our littleness, love to feel nothing, then we shall be poor in spirit, and Jesus will come to us, *far off* as we are, He will transform us in love's flames. It is trust and nothing but trust, that must bring us to Love. Fear brings us only to Justice.[41]

The task is no longer difficult

We are taken from our Egyptian captivity and set free in Jesus and carried in the arms of Love. Then it does not matter whether we travel in desert or soft country, for he provides and carries, all in his action alone. 'Yahweh your God goes ahead of you and will be fighting on your side just as you saw him in Egypt. You have seen him in the desert too: Yahweh your God continued to support you as a man supports his son, all along the road you followed until you arrived here.'[42]

Thérèse further commented upon the complete trust in God which is entailed:

> From the moment I understood that it was impossible for me to do anything by myself, the task imposed upon me no longer appeared difficult. I felt that the only thing necessary was to unite myself more and more to Jesus and that 'all these things will be given to you besides.'[43] In fact never was my hope mistaken, for God saw fit to fill my little hand as many times as it was necessary.[44]

Good news does not make secular newspaper headlines, but as 'cold water to a thirsty throat, such is good news from a distant land.'[45] The saints are good news of the kingdom; they have trusted in the actions of God's love, as did Thérèse, and their experience is living proof of the efficacy of tranquil trust in God's love amid trials. The saints are an invitation to us to get involved and emulate them. We have the example, among countless others, of the peaceful trust of St Maximilian Kolbe, the Polish Franciscan who founded a community near Warsaw which combined prayer with cheerfulness and poverty with modern technology. His community produced weekly and daily papers. After the German invasion of Poland, he was interned and then released. Whereupon he went back to his monastery and turned it into a refugee camp housing nearly five thousand displaced Jews and other Poles. Eventually he was arrested and sent to Auschwitz with other brothers.

He maintained his priestly ministry secretly in the camp and brought comfort and compassion to the most afflicted, within the most degraded and bestial of conditions it is possible for human evil to create. Following the escape to freedom of one of the prisoners, the Germans, according to the normal rules in such a case, required ten prisoners from the hut of the escapee to be chosen, and then taken to a special bunker where they were left to thirst and starve to death. Such a mode of death is one of the very most terrible, painful ways known. The Romans lashed their prisoners for crucifixion before the nailing, to ensure that the weakened man died the sooner, and so suffer that much less. No such mercy was shown by the German jailers. Father Maximilian offered to replace one of the younger terrified prisoners who had been chosen for the torment. This the Germans accepted, and he was led away with the other nine prisoners to the special bunker.

Then the miracle of transfiguration of suffering began. A German guard afterwards described the atmosphere of the darkened death bunker as becoming like that of a cathedral full of light, for Maximilian tenderly gathered the incarcerated prisoners and led them in prayers and the singing of psalms, as he prepared them for a dignified, faith-filled Passion. After a fortnight four prisoners were still alive, and Maximilian was still conscious. He was finally despatched by an injection of phenol, on the 14th August 1941. The prisoner he had saved attended the service in 1982 in which Maximilian Kolbe was recognized as a saint and placed on the Roman Calendar of canonized saints.

Deprivation within material affluence

While this book was being written, there has been a remarkable event on radio, when the third symphony of the contemporary Polish composer Henryk Górecki remained for a very protracted period in the classical music top ten, decided by the level of purchases of the recorded music sold via a national book and recorded music retailer. This symphony is entitled a *Symphony of Sorrowful Songs*. Clearly, its tranquil expression of sorrow and suffering, in an extended composition, struck the hearts and minds of a huge number of listeners. Was it that the music was a significant expression, and cathartic exploration, of the silent, often unseen, awareness of suffering of many 'ordinary' people we see round us in the streets each day? Was this reaction to this music a measure of the deprivation present in a material affluence which cannot fill the emptiness which only poverty of spirit can fulfil [46]—an affluence which needs the poverty of the One who has nowhere to lay his head[47] except in us?

Certainly, the music relates human suffering to the Suffering, the Passion of Christ and so covers and infuses human suffering, if we but will, with a dignity and significance which is cosmic, and so, bearable because greater than us. The music relates suffering to our salvation and so ends in rising and expectant tones. The symphony includes a setting of the following words, written on the wall of cell number three of the basement of the *Palace*, the Gestapo's headquarters in Zakopane, Poland. Beneath is the signature of Helena Wanda Blazusiakówna and the words '18 years old, imprisoned since 26 September 1944:'

> No, Mother, do not weep,
> Most chaste Queen of Heaven
> Support me always.
> Zdrowas Mario (Ave Maria)[48]

In such suffering love there is no anger or hate, just patience and hope; and a miraculous trust in the actions of God's limitless love — 'support me always.' And that trusting departure from self which is in Helena's comforting of the Mother of God — 'Mother, do not weep.' Did not Jesus say, love your enemy, so that we may be children of our Father in heaven?[49] This saying by Thérèse is relevant:

> How great a soul must be to be able to contain a God. Yet the soul of a *day-old* child is for Him a paradise of delights; what then will our souls be, that have fought and suffered?[50]

This is not an argument for supine acceptance of suffering and pain, for suffering inflicted in evil intent is of the rebellious angel who fell from grace; it is our task to combat such evil. But we are free to rise with Jesus to transmute and sanctify, through him, by his power, that suffering which persists despite our proper and reasonable efforts to allay and ease suffering. That is a calling to the dignity of the graced children of God whereby Jesus works in us to bring to him all his scattered and confused creatures. The Christian attitude to pain and suffering is realistic and it is healing, it is truth. It was at the core of Jesus' teaching, as Thérèse emphasized:

> To keep Jesus' *word*—that is the sole condition of our happiness, the proof of our love for Him. But what *is* this word? Praying to His Father for His disciples, He expresses Himself thus: 'Sanctify them by thy *word*, thy word is *truth.*'[51] We know then what the *Word* is that we must keep; we do not, like Pilate, ask Jesus 'What is truth?'[52] We possess *Truth*, we *keep* Jesus in our *hearts.* How sweet it will be one day to hear that most loving word proceed from Jesus' mouth: 'And you are they who have continued with me in my temptations: and I dispose to you, as my Father has disposed to me, a kingdom!'[53] The temptations of Jesus, what mystery is there. So He too has His temptations! He has indeed. And often He *'treads the winepress alone.* He

seeks for those who may give him aid and finds none.'[54] Many serve Jesus when He consoles them, few are willing to keep company with Jesus sleeping on the waves *or suffering in the garden of agony!*[55]

Then we can become like Helena, patient and trusting, unknown, unseen, who even in her own suffering seeks only to comfort and console the heaven which weeps over her. Is that not being vigorous, hale and healed, and holy? Is that not being that to which one is called, being a little unseen saint, trusting quietly with miraculous tranquillity in the actions of God's limitless love, even in the pit? 'Even if I were to walk in a ravine as dark as death I should fear no danger, for you are at my side.'[56]

The little way in darkness

Trust cannot be truly experienced and known until there is cause for it amid unknowing faith. But most of our lives, if not all, contain periods when such trust is called for and can always be realized if we will. Thérèse knew this little way of tranquil trust in a darkness which was with her for the last seven years of her life:

Then Jesus took me by the hand and brought me into a subterranean way, where it was neither hot nor cold, where the sun does not shine, and rain and wind do not come; a tunnel where I see nothing but a brightness half-veiled, the glow from the downcast eyes in the Face of my Spouse.

My Spouse says nothing to me, nor do I say anything to Him either, save that *I love Him* more than *myself*, and in the depth of my heart I feel this is true, for I am more His than my own!

I do not see that we are advancing towards the mountain that is our goal, because our journey is under the earth; yet I have a feeling that we are approaching it, without knowing why.

The road I follow is one of no consolation for me, yet it brings me all consolations because it is Jesus who has chosen it, and I desire to console Him only.[57]

During the last year of her life the darkness thickened and she descended into a night of doubt and disbelief, which she endured redemptively for unbelievers while steadfastly maintaining faith, for had not Jesus himself cried from the cross: 'My God, why have you forsaken me?'

Then suddenly the fog which surrounds me becomes more dense; it penetrates my soul and envelops it in such a way that it is impossible to discover within it the sweet image of my Fatherland; everything has disappeared! When I want to rest my heart fatigued by the darkness which surrounds it by the memory of the luminous country after which I aspire, my torment redoubles. . . . He knows very well that while I do not have *the joy of faith*, I am trying to carry out its works at least.[58]

But Thérèse also states her firm belief that Jesus matches his action in each of us with our particular capability:

How sweet and merciful the Lord really is, for He did not send me this trial until the moment I was capable of bearing it. A little earlier I believe it would have plunged me into a state of discouragement.[59]

To go down into the waters of rebirth, to be washed and remade requires our leap in tranquil trust — in darkness but also in trust, like a Helena. We can, as a Thérèse, in this pilgrimage trust in the supportive company of the communion of saints which Jesus gives us as his promised kingdom:

I believe that the Blessed in Heaven have a great compassion for our wretchedness; they remember that when they were frail and mortal like us they committed the same faults, endured the same struggles, and their fraternal love becomes greater even than it was on earth, which is why they do not cease to protect us and pray for us.[60]

Thérèse further commented:

> What a joy it is to think that God is Just, i.e.,
> that He takes into account our weakness, that
> He is perfectly aware of our fragile nature.
> What should I fear then?[61]

The tired, sick man nursed by Mother Teresa was claimed gently by Jesus as she washed him. Little children who do not struggle as they are washed find it so easy, and may even be surprised that it is enjoyable, and they are able to smile. If we hesitate before the seeming cataclysm of a leap in blind, trusting faith, then we can remember that the word *cataclysm* stems from the Greek for to *wash* and for *flood*. The imagery becomes rich. The suffering Hindu, the poorest of the poor, already poor in spirit and therefore blessed by Jesus,[62] smiled as he underwent his cataclysmic washing, flooded by peace as his pain ceased. In Jesus' littlest and poorest, he is praised.[63] Will he not be as gentle with us, who have so much more, if we are but as accepting?

> For I shall take you from among the nations
> and gather you back from all the countries,
> and bring you home to your own country.
> I shall pour clean water over you
> and you will be cleansed [64]

Remaining in the present moment

We accept and leap, and then discern what Jesus wills to do. Committing the past to his covering and forgiving mercy, which forgets what was in the contrition of the now, we leave to Jesus the future and simply remain in the present moment, the now. As Thérèse pointed out:

> We who run in the way of love shouldn't be thinking of sufferings that can take place in the future; it's a lack of confidence, it's like meddling in the work of creation.[65]

She has already assured us that if we had in the past committed all the sins possible, we should simply go heartbroken to Jesus and throw ourselves in his arms.

Georges Bernanos commented that it is often a leap taken in despair that throws us into hopeful trust and confidence. In some lives it is an essential first step. If one is angry and perplexed, then express it! Howl at heaven! The psalms may be used, for they cover the whole gamut of human emotions from joy to deep puzzlement and agony. They hold many expressions of human pain, perplexity and anger. Some of these verses can be said in disbelief and fury; they become then very alive and real, and Jesus responds to that. Jesus was angry on occasion; anger can be holy, or at least point the way to healing and holiness. Jesus wished us either cold or hot—only lukewarmness is rejected.[66] He wants us to be real, not to feign feelings or attitudes which are not for real. As Thérèse said, there is no room for pretence in the little way. Jesus may have invited us to rest in him, but coming to Jesus more often seems like a wrestling not a resting. Jesus can take anger and transfigure it. It is just that we diagnose the cause of our anger wrongly. He can handle that. He was the step-son of a carpenter. The pumpkin is not changed into a coach without a lot of celestial carpentry, radical re-making and some noise. Pumpkins may rest where they are, but a coach is made to move, and we need to move from where we are, or rather, be moved.

In all situations Jesus is there and there is always aid; as Thérèse commented:

> Think! We did not dare even to look at ourselves, so utterly dull and unadorned we felt: and Jesus calls us. He wants to gaze on us in leisure, but He is not alone, with Him come the other two Persons of the Blessed Trinity to take possession of our soul. Jesus promised it long ago when He was on the point of ascending to *His Father and our Father.*[67] He said with tenderness unutterable: 'If anyone love me, he will keep my word and my Father will love him and we will come to him and will make our abode with him.'[68]

Finally flooded with trust

One day Augustine of Hippo listened to a visiting friend describe the radical decision of two young men who were employed at the court of the Emperor. The

young men had come upon the story of the life of St
Anthony who was the pioneer of the Desert Fathers
whose sayings we have briefly looked at. One of the
young men, after reading, and deeply moved, was filled
with anger at himself. Suddenly he turned to the other
and said, 'What are we looking for? What is our
purpose in serving the State? Can we hope for anything
better at Court than to be the Emperor's friends? . . .
But if I wish it I can become the friend of God at this
very moment!' Augustine then further writes of this
young man, 'After saying this he turned back to the
book, labouring under the pain of the new life that was
taking birth in him. He read on . . . his heart leaping . . .
a cry broke from him as he saw the better course and
determined to take it.'

Under the pain of new life being born in him—anger—the
heart leaping—a cry forced from him. Once more the
process of conversion is seen as a radical departure. The
young man and his companion decided to become
Christians and to let this fundamentally affect their
lives.

Augustine himself at that time was in travail. He was
a man of the heart, passionate and warm-blooded.
Born in 354 AD in Thagaste in what is now Algeria, he
was brought up as a Christian (though not baptized) by
a pagan father and a Christian mother, St Monica. He
had studied rhetoric, the art of persuasive speaking, to
become a lawyer; then philosophy. Living in the
Roman empire shortly after Christianity had been
finally accepted by Emperor Constantine and adopted
as the State religion, Augustine travelled from

Carthage in North Africa where he attended university, to Rome and Milan where he taught rhetoric. In the course of all this Augustine deserted his childhood Christianity.

Following a long, painful inner struggle, Augustine returned to Christianity in 386 and was baptized. Back in North Africa, he followed a semi-monastic life with some friends. In 391 he was ordained priest. Only another five years later he was to be the bishop of Hippo. He led in a warm-hearted and supportive manner. St Augustine of Hippo is an intellectual giant in the whole history of our civilization; his influence on Christian thought is among the foremost.

His conversion story is told in his *Confessions*. It is compelling reading, showing the path of his life through the hesitant course of his conversion. He wrestled against Jesus, and only after prolonged struggle and great difficulty did he come to a new way of life in Christianity. Augustine writes of his delayed, problem-filled approach to Jesus' call to him. In his departure from his old self, he says that God put him, Augustine, before himself so that he saw his own state. He was being turned around, he was placed in a revolution so that he could see that, as he was, there was no escape from himself. We have looked at this trapping of self within self before, in our present exploration. He experienced a stripping of self — 'I stood naked before my own eyes.' His self finally exhausted all its old arguments against simply capitulating and following God, and 'stood silent and afraid'—for the pangs of a rebirth were already present.

'My inner house was a house divided against itself . . . my looks betrayed the commotion in my mind as I exclaimed, What is the matter with us . . . then my feelings proved too strong for me.' Augustine then describes how in inner agitation he went into his garden for privacy while he was in struggle within himself as his own fierce contender:

> I *was beside myself* with madness that would bring me sanity. I was *dying a death that would bring me life.* I knew the evil that was in me, but the good that was soon to be born in me I did not know. . . . I was frantic, overcome by *violent anger* with myself for not accepting Your will and entering into Your covenant . . . I was held back by mere trifles, the most paltry inanities, all my old attachments. They plucked at my garment of flesh and whispered, 'Are you going to dismiss us? From this moment we shall never be with you again, for ever and ever . . .' I had much to say to You, my God, not in these very words but in this strain: Lord, will you never be content? Must we always taste Your vengeance? . . . weeping all the while with the most bitter sorrow in my heart, when all at once I heard the singing voice of a child in a nearby house. Whether it was the voice of a boy or girl I cannot say, but again and again it repeated the refrain 'Take it and read, take it and read.' At this I looked up, thinking hard whether

there was any kind of game in which children used to chant words like these, but I could not remember ever hearing them before. I stemmed my flood of tears and stood up, telling myself that this could only be a divine command to open my book of Scripture and read the first passage on which my eyes should fall. . . . I seized it and opened it, and in silence I read the first passage on which my eyes fell: 'Not in revelling and drunkenness, not in lust and wantonness, not in quarrels and rivalries. Rather, arm yourselves with the Lord Jesus Christ; spend no more thought on nature and on nature's appetites.'[69] For in an instant, as I came to the end of the sentence, it was as though the *light of confidence flooded into my heart* and all the darkness of doubt was dispelled.[70]

So, finally *flooded* with the light of confidence and trust, with doubt dispelled, Augustine turns from self and is released to new life and fruitfulness. The Hound of Heaven has triumphed, and holding his prize by the hand, takes him with him.

Special lights burning in the firmament

Near the end of his *Confessions,* Augustine says to God, 'You set special lights to burn in the firmament. These were your saints, who are possessed of the Word which gives life. In them there shines the sublime authority that is conferred upon them by their spiritual gifts.' [71]

The fruit of his rebirth is shown through the intense language and imagery of trusting love with which Augustine lights his writings, and so lights our lives and re-awakens hope of the transmutation and the resolution of struggle in a flooding of peace:

> I have learnt to love you late, Beauty at once so ancient and so new! I have learnt to love you late! You were within me, and I was in the world outside myself. I searched for you outside myself and, disfigured as I was, I fell upon the lovely things of your creation. You were with me, but I was not with you. You shone upon me; your radiance enveloped me; you put my blindness to flight. I tasted you and now I hunger and thirst for you. You touched me and I am inflamed with love of your peace.[72]

We have read the words from Hosea of the Old Testament which describe God's welcome to the returning one who has been unfaithful—I will betroth you to myself for ever, I will betroth you in uprightness and justice, and faithful love and tenderness and in the knowledge of Yahweh. It is impossible in this world for us to comprehend God's love completely. Three months before his death, after a lifetime as a luminary whose scholarship and teaching was given special honour and attention at the great reforming Council of Trent, St Thomas Aquinas had a spiritual experience of God from which Thomas could write no more. For, he said, what he had seen had made all his work seem so

much straw. Thérèse would have commented that all
we can ever offer to the Fire of Love are little straws, for
love itself is the fuel of Love.

The closeness of intimate love

As we read the Word of God he speaks to us even in
terms reflecting our experience of the closest and most
intimate of human loves. In the Song of Songs we read a
mirroring of Divine Love which uses the language of the
relationship of lover and beloved, between husband and
wife. Thérèse was familiar with this book in the Bible and
drew from it to express her understanding of the love
which God is for each and every one of us. She also
described a particular experience she had shortly after she
had especially offered herself and her life to love, to be
Love, and her description conveys something of the
ultimately inexpressible, that which hunts and hounds us
to possess us. She was praying the Stations of the Way of
the Cross:

> Suddenly, I was seized with such a violent love
> for God that I can't explain it except by saying
> it felt as though I were totally plunged into
> fire. Oh! What fire and what sweetness at one
> and the same time! I was on fire with love, and
> I felt that one minute more, one second more,
> and I wouldn't be able to sustain this ardour
> without dying. I understood then what the
> saints were saying about these states which
> they experienced so often. As for me, I experi-

enced it only once and for one single instant, falling back immediately into my habitual state of dryness.[73]

Love cannot offer other than complete, unconditioned love within the child's unconditional acceptance. Sister Marie of the Trinity spoke about the repeatedly stated belief of Thérèse that Jesus reserves his privileges for little ones, urging the trust, self-surrender, simplicity, uprightness, and humility of the child — 'give yourself up to him without fear.'[74] Thérèse was vowed in religious life to Jesus as her Spouse. He is the Betrothed, the Promised True One, of each and every one who turns to him and accepts him without conditions, trusting him in all things — *I will betroth you to myself for ever with tenderness and love; and you will come to know Yahweh.* Thérèse's absolute trust in Jesus and in his action, a trust held despite trial and tribulation in serenity and tranquillity, is example and proof of that to which we all are called and drawn. 'Nobody can frighten me because I know where I stand in His love and mercy.'

The little child knows that Jesus acts within it,
inspiring it in all he desires it to do at each moment.
Following the way of confidence and total abandon,
it is happy only to do the will of God.
Knowing that it is Jesus' hand that governs all,
in everything the child sees only Jesus,
knowing that it is trust and nothing but trust
that will bring it to Love
and that God does not disappoint a trust
so filled with humility.

Chapter 5

Persistence in prayer as a simple raising of the heart to God

I do like children who do not know how to read, I say very simply to God what I wish to say, without composing beautiful sentences, and He always understands me. For me, prayer is an aspiration of the heart, it is a simple glance directed to Heaven, it is a cry of gratitude and love in the midst of trial as well as joy; finally, it is something great, supernatural, which expands my soul and unites me to Jesus.

St Thérèse, *Story of a Soul*, Ch. XI, p. 242

Thérèse, when asked how she had reached her peace, replied that she had forgotten self and was careful to seek herself in nothing.[1] In her thoughtlessness for herself in her needs, she found peace in forgetting self. Prayer, so often thought by us as a means of asking, was for her a means of giving. When the beloved sits with the loved one, the heart wishes only to adore and offer love—not to seek self, but to centre upon the other and the love shared between two hearts.

The instinctive action of the simplest child in peaceful happiness with its parent is to press itself to its mother and express its love of her, knowing that all

comes from her and that she knows all its needs. God
meets childlike need, not childish want. Before ever the
heart of his child is awakened towards him, there is
utter assurance that 'He has given his angels orders
about you, to guard you wherever you go. Since he
clings to me I rescue him . . . in distress I am at his
side.'[2] Saint Catherine of Siena thanked the Father for
having given those things which she never sought and
never realized she needed — much, much more than
she ever thought to ask for.

This responsive divine action is itself a mould in
which belief and trust are cast. In time the first
hesitant, even doubting, call can change and grow into
the habitual prayer of trust of the open, vulnerable
heart centred on God in directness and simplicity. The
best kind of prayer, commented St Francis de Sales, is
that in which with simplicity of heart our mind is
centred on God and we neither think about ourselves
nor what we are doing. The *Catechism of the Catholic
Church* speaks of our heart:

> The heart is the dwelling place where I am,
> where I live. The heart is our hidden centre,
> beyond the grasp of our reason and of others;
> only the Spirit of God can fathom our human
> heart and know it fully. The heart is the place
> of decision, deeper than our psychic drives. It
> is the place of truth, where we choose life or
> death. It is the place of encounter, because as
> image of God we live in relation: it is the place
> of covenant.[3]

For Thérèse, prayer is the yearning heart, simple and direct in utter dependency; it is the place of truthful encounter where we choose life in a real relationship in unity with Jesus:

> For me, prayer is an aspiration of the heart, it is a simple glance directed to Heaven, it is a cry of love and gratitude in the midst of trial as well as joy; finally, it is something great, supernatural, which expands my soul and unites me to Jesus.[4]

Short prayer penetrates heaven

This spirit of dependency, directness and simplicity was stressed by the writer of *The Cloud of Unknowing* which was written as a manual of prayer during the latter half of the fourteenth century. The unknown English author discusses a particular mode of prayer called contemplative, but we need not be distracted by, nor caught up in, labels and preconceptions. The author's point which catches our attention is relevant for the continuing prayer of humility, directness, simplicity and dependency. The dependency of the child in its turning towards the parent does of course nevertheless contain a world of total need. Self-forgetfulness does not eradicate need but is grounded on a fundamental trust in the sole intention of the parent to anticipate and meet all the needs of the child, which are many. So,

the attention of the child moves from itself to the pro-
vider for all needs, and to the reciprocation of love.

The Cloud of Unknowing describes the reaction of a
person caught by fright caused in any sudden
threatening incident. The urgency of the situation
leads to the use of few words in a bare, stripped cry of
'Help!' This, he says, is why it is written *short prayer
penetrates heaven.* Jesus said, in prayer do not babble, do
not use many words.[5] This bare simplicity pierces
through to God more quickly than any long prayer
centred on self and recited without real involvement:

> Why does it penetrate Heaven, this short little
> prayer of one syllable? Surely because it is
> prayed with a full heart, in the height and
> depth and length and breadth of the spirit of
> him that prays it. No wonder that a soul
> moulded by grace into the close image and
> likeness of God his maker is so soon heard by
> God! Yes, even if it is a very sinful soul, who is
> as it were an enemy of God. If he through grace
> were to cry such a short syllable in the height,
> depth and length and breadth of his spirit, he
> would always be heard because of this
> anguished cry, and be helped by God . . . what
> pity and mercy shall God have for the spiritual
> cry of a soul that comes from its height and
> depth and length and breadth![6]

We know for sure that none — neither the doubter
nor the believer — turn to God without already being

enfolded within the Holy Spirit,[7] inspired by the Spirit to make that cry. The cry itself is the first fruits of the prevenient and certain action of God. We are promised by Jesus that if we turn and remain with him, we can ask in our need for whatever we please.[8] That, of course, does not mean that we are free to demand childishly. Meaningful prayer, true prayer from our true heart, is the action of the Holy Spirit. Our true heart is the temple of the Holy Spirit [9] who cries out on our behalf in our inability and who provides according to the mind of God in our poverty.[10]

God supplies for my weakness

Speaking of the visits by her sister Cèline (named Sister Geneviève on her entry to Carmel) when Cèline was taking care of her ill father, Thérèse shows in a practical way how this prayerful dependence on God's action, this centredness on God, can replace our own unprayerful worrying and doing:

> When Sister Geneviève used to come to visit me, I wasn't able to say all I wanted to say in a half hour. Then, during the week, whenever I had a thought or else was sorry for having forgotten to tell her something, I would ask God to let her know and understand what I was thinking about, and in the next visit she'd speak to me exactly about the thing I had asked God to let her know.

At the beginning, when she was really suffering and I was unable to console her, I would leave the visit with a heavy heart, but I soon understood it wasn't I who could console anyone; and then I was no longer troubled when she left very sad. I begged God to supply for my weakness, and I felt He answered me. I would see this in the following visit. Since that time, whenever I involuntarily caused anyone any trouble, I would beg God to repair it, and then I no longer torment myself with the matter.[11]

Thérèse lost complexity, torment and heaviness of heart; she found ease and simplicity of heart in prayerful, trusting dependence on God. 'I shall give you a new heart, and put a new spirit in you; I shall remove the heart of stone from your bodies and give you a heart of flesh instead. I shall put my spirit in you,' God promises.[12]

Prayer is a turning to God in which the individual is enabled to turn responsively to the call which God has already made to his child from whom he has never turned away. This call is in every one of his children, no matter their condition, place or belief as such — the infant able to only makes cries, the person in primitive life, these the wild flowers whose simplicity attracts him, as Thérèse expressed it—each is offered his or her own singular and personal relationship and life with him. The essential way remains the same, but each relationship can mature into one different in genius (that is, the endowed creative power given freely by the

Father to the child through Jesus in the Holy Spirit) from all others. But such gifting and maturation is always grounded and rooted in prayer — in the heart open to the action of the Holy Spirit.

A little way of creative freedom

In that openness the Holy Spirit is free to act as he wills. Thérèse underlines the fact that the little way she has discovered is not a set of new rules and regulations with which to constrict oneself or others into a preconceived common mould:

> One feels that to do good is as impossible without God's help as to make the sun shine at night. One feels it absolutely necessary to forget one's likings, one's personal conceptions, and to guide souls along the road which Jesus has traced out for them without trying to make them walk one's own way.[13]

For Thérèse, prayer is a little way of creative freedom, of spiritual space and openness, a little way of adventure, of renewal and of trust within tranquillity—because it is not a human action but the action of Jesus, the one who came to set his children free from the bondage of Egypt. 'The Spirit which gives life in Christ Jesus has set you free.'[14]

Thérèse's approach to prayer remains always simple and direct, devoid of complexity or composed methodology. Her simplicity is entirely consistent with her decision in her very heart to choose life through littleness and inability. This simplicity precludes reliance upon any involved method of meditation. It is not that she is ignorant of the complexities and stages of progress in prayer elaborated by the various spiritual writers; far from it, but she rejects them for a way which is short and direct:

> How great is the power of *Prayer!* One could call it a Queen who has at each instant free access to the King and who is able to obtain whatever she asks. To be heard it is not necessary to read from a book some *beautiful* formula composed for the occasion. If this were the case, alas, I would have to be pitied! Outside the Divine Office which I am very unworthy to recite, I do not have the courage to force myself to search out beautiful prayers in books. There are so many of them it really gives me a headache! Each prayer is more beautiful than the others. I cannot recite them all and not knowing which to choose, I do like children who do not know how to read, I say to God very simply what I wish to say, without composing beautiful sentences, and He always understands me.[15]

To Thérèse prayer is a living relationship, a relationship in which the child acts naturally and normally, expressing itself without a false inhibition learned from sophisticated adults. Her prayer is a spontaneous, unforced personal impulse, coming from the heart of love. 'How good our Jesus is! How sweet it is to confide in him!' she gratefully exclaimed on receiving an answer to a prayer in need.[16] Prayer then is a pulse of the heart, essential for its well-being and natural to its loving nature. 'As for the man who has not begun to pray, I beg him for the love of God not to forgo this great blessing. Here is no place for fear, only for desire . . . no one ever took His Majesty for a friend without receiving a reward,' wrote Teresa of Avila. 'However sinful a man may be, he should not abandon prayer.'[17]

Sin is a disabling burden, a self-inflicted division between us and God from which we suffer in our self-deprivation. It is our refusal of that Love which nevertheless is always present to us and is always offered passionately to us. Since sin is an injury and a deprivation, a spiritual suicide, it has a symptom, the pain it causes. That pain is in the rupture of the proper relationship with God; prayer is the repairing of that relationship. Prayer enables a growing sensitiveness to God in listening and responding to him; for God has never ceased praying to us and so enabling us to turn to him and pray to him. In prayer, we give room for God to work to restore our proper relationship with him.

Avoid needless worry and scrupulosity

In the building of that close relationship we will be very aware that we come to Jesus from sin. But we can become increasingly aware within our heart that we have been released in a very real way from the slavery of sin. We will wish so deeply, within our heart, to solely please Jesus and give joy to him. We have already read in an earlier chapter Thérèse's assurance to her cousin that the one who wants to belong entirely to Jesus cannot be made to sin by the devil, who can only make the little one believe it has sinned. This level of assurance given to us by Thérèse must be singular among the saints. It is an assurance firmly rooted in Scripture and can profitably be kept well in mind, to avoid needless worry and scrupulosity. In our weakness and littleness our heart is now wholly vulnerable to God, and while fault and failure will no doubt recur no real damage can be done by involuntary mistakes. In reply to her sister Pauline, Mother Agnes of Jesus, who was confiding to her some thoughts of sorrow and discouragement after having committed a fault, Thérèse firmly said:

> You don't act like me. When I commit a fault that makes me sad, I know very well that this sadness is a consequence of my infidelity, but do you believe I remain there? Oh! no, I'm not so foolish! I hasten to say to God: My God, I know I have merited this feeling of sadness, but let me offer it up to You just the same as a trial that You sent me through love. I'm sorry for my sin, but I'm happy to have this suffering to offer to You.[18]

We need not be tormented by these failures, they are not a burden if we have cast our sinful self, our refusal of life, onto the cross of Jesus and into his Tomb. Jesus took our sin upon himself,[19] and therefore we are free to be truly in him in new life — re-born in the Holy Spirit—free from the slavery of sin. Our burden, if we but will, will fall from us; so we are released, dead to the old burden.[20] Thus, we move even now into the perpetual Easter of the Resurrection; through prayer we are raised to life, bound into the risen life of Jesus himself.

Then, in our release we can cry in short, loving prayer: *Abba*, Father![21] as children of God. We are still crying 'help!' But now in a renewed, trusting and calm state, learning that all prayer is answered, even if in a way and at a time not always convenient to our limited outlook and preconceptions. 'Must here be the beginning of my bliss?. . . Blessed rather be the Man who was put to shame for me!' as John Bunyan expressed it in his *Pilgrim's Progress.*

The Cloud of Unknowing speaks of the breaking out, the overflowing of the soul into 'some appropriate word of good, such as "Good Jesus!" "Lovely Jesus!" "Sweet Jesus!" and so on' springing from spiritual gladness.[22] Thérèse used the fond title, *Papa* God. She commented that she accepted everything out of love for God, even all sorts of extravagant thoughts.[23] It is this uncalculated directness and spontaneity which Thérèse teaches us to use. We then break out of our inhibitions and the bondage of distant, fearful awe, the products of our fallen state, the old Adam in us. Jesus spoke of our *Abba;*[24] thus with an Aramaic word he expresses the close familiarity — the intimate family union—of Son with Father, of his Child with God. He spoke in an agony of heart just before his Passion which was to gather up all our little passions to be baptized into his death, and so deliver us from the bondage of death and sin once and for all. Following the examples of Jesus and Thérèse, we ourselves can speak those titles with confidence and gratitude in familiar closeness to him in his sharing of his love.

Sharing with the world

Love is unreserved sharing. In it we share our salvation with the world and in that sharing we share the life of the world. We cannot go to God alone, but only in the company of the communion of saints which is the Church suffering, the Church militant and dynamic, and the Church triumphant. Love is unreserved sharing within the family of the saints, among whom we are now embraced and included. Thérèse commented:

> Very often, without our knowing it, the graces and lights we receive are due to a hidden soul, for God wills that the saints communicate grace to each other through prayer with great love, with a love much greater than that of a family, and even the most perfect family on earth. How often have I thought that I may owe all the graces I've received to the prayers of a person who begged them from God for me, and whom I shall know only in Heaven.[25]

When we pray, even when alone in a desert, every heavenly soul and angel bends over us and joins with us. We pray from within the communion of saints, whether we are praying in community or personally. In a very fundamental sense there is no such thing as private prayer. When we pray when physically alone we pray in and through the Holy Spirit, and so within the Body of Christ, the Church visible and invisible, the community of prayer. This means that even the troubled doubter turning in a cry of travail to the hoped-for God is already led by the Holy Spirit in praying from within the invisible wider ramparts of the Church, from within the Body of Christ. 'The Spirit too comes to help us in our weakness, for, when we do not know how to pray properly, then the Spirit personally makes our petitions for us in groans that cannot be put into words; and he who can see into all hearts knows what the Spirit means . . . and turns everything to their good.'[26]

Discussing her prayer for those missionaries for whom she had been given a special responsibility of spiritual care and with whom she corresponded and gave encouragement and advice, Thérèse reflects this community aspect and action of prayer: 'How could I not pray for the souls whom they will save in their distant mission through suffering and preaching?' Then she takes the thought further:

Jesus says that everything we ask the *Father in His Name,* He will grant it.[27] No doubt, it is because of this teaching that the Holy Spirit, before Jesus' birth, dictated this prophetic prayer: *Draw me, we shall run.*[28] What is it then to ask to be *drawn* if not to be united in an intimate way to the object which captivates our heart? I ask Jesus to draw me into the flames of His love, to unite me so closely with Him that He live and act in me, (then) the more I shall say *'Draw me'* the more also these souls (for whom she prays) will run swiftly in the odour of the ointments of their Beloved, for a soul that is burning with love cannot remain inactive.[29]

Thérèse is teaching us her understanding of prayer as community, and prayer as action. So often prayer is seen as a retreat, a withdrawal from the world. In a certain sense this is so. But nevertheless the essence of prayer is an advance into the community of prayer and a facing towards the world. In heaven we shall be in the fruition of the communion of saints and we shall not ever then wish to love God alone and withdrawn, for love is the eternal fullness of sharing. Prayer draws us into Jesus' life and action, and so into his love encompassing all human needs. In such a perspective, when we pray we go out to meet the world and to give the world the life of Jesus. Thérèse, a strictly enclosed nun, was called to be a missionary in a life devoted to prayer. She has been declared by the Church as patroness of the missions. Prayer of its very nature is missionary and reaches out and encompasses all in love:

All the saints have understood this, and more especially those who filled the world with the light of the Gospel teachings. Was it not in prayer that St Paul, St Augustine, St John of the Cross, St Thomas Aquinas, St Francis, St Dominic, and so many other famous Friends of God have drawn out this divine science which delights the greatest geniuses? A scholar has said: *'Give me a lever and I will lift the world.'* What Archimedes was not able to obtain, for his request was not directed by God and was only made from a material viewpoint, the saints have obtained in all its fullness. The Almighty has given them as *fulcrum:* HIMSELF ALONE; as *lever:* PRAYER which burns with a fire of love. And it is in this way that they have *lifted the world;* it is in this way that the saints still militant lift it, and that, until the end of time, the saints to come will lift it.[30]

A new centredness on others

Thérèse was acutely aware of this dynamism of prayer which takes us out of self to a new centredness on others through the Other, Jesus; she catches us up in the ambition to join forces in covering those we do not know, but whom we can reach through Jesus' Spirit:

We must not grow weary of praying. Confidence works miracles and Jesus told

Blessed Margaret Mary: *'One just soul* has so
much power over my Heart that it can obtain
from it pardon for a *thousand criminals.'* No one
knows whether he himself is just or sinful, but
Jesus gives us the grace to feel in the very depth
of our heart that we would rather die than
offend Him. And in any event it is not our
merits but those of our Spouse, which are ours,
that we offer to our Father who is in heaven.[31]

*The Spirit comes to help us in our weakness, for, when we do
not know how to pray properly, then the Spirit personally
makes our petitions for us. . . .* When his disciples asked
Jesus to teach them how to pray, it was not because
they did not already pray, for they were good Jews
taking their religion seriously within the then most
venerable and wisest of traditions. Indeed, they already
had made great sacrifice to serve God. But they saw
something about Jesus and his relationship with his
Father; a quality of directness, dependency and
simplicity. He is alone among the teachers of the great
religious traditions in speaking about God our Father
in such familiarly intimate, trusting and loving terms.
The disciples saw all this, and so in effect were wanting
to learn to pray all over again. They wanted to learn to
pray from the master of prayer. Jesus then taught them
not to babble a lot of words but to be dependent and in
simplicity. He taught them that our *Abba* Father
already knows what we need before we do ourselves.
He taught a prayer which consists of just fifty-nine
words and which covers all needs:

Our Father in heaven,
may your name be held holy,
your kingdom come,
your will be done,
on earth as in heaven.
Give us today our daily bread.
And forgive us our debts
as we have forgiven those who are in debt to
us.
And do not put us to the test,
but save us from the Evil One.[32]

Only *one* clause of the prayer is conditional — *if* we forgive others then we *will* be forgiven. *When* we have forgiven — and surely we can only intently desire that which only God can fully do, in us and for us — we *are* forgiven. *As* we forgive, we *are* forgiven. 'Do not judge, and you will not be judged; because the judgements you give are the judgements you will get, and the standard you use will be the standard used for you,' Jesus taught.[33]

There is a very important aspect of Thérèse's teaching which seems sometimes to be overlooked. In choosing divine Love before Justice, and in offering herself to Love completely, Thérèse opted to avoid judgement of herself by God, and so avoided judgement of others, preferring to see and think about their good intentions and aspirations rather than dwell on their actions, even if these had been unfortunate and troublesome. She knew that the fruition of love is devoid of judgement but is wholly a consummation of fervent acceptance and unification. It is the fullness of sharing in which judgement as we normally understand that term becomes irrelevant. That is surely why Jesus asks us to say that conditional clause in his prayer, and to say it thoughtfully and carefully. We shall receive just that measure we have given. There is *no* judgement for those who do *not* judge.

Not to judge someone is to love them, without reserve in a full sharing of love, even those who do us harm and are enemies. *I do not even judge myself,*[34] but I seek only to please Jesus, to console him and give him joy. All else is his concern, his will, for which we pray: 'Your will be done on earth as it is in heaven.' Then the Kingdom of heaven is given to those who will produce its fruit.[35]

> I really don't see what I'll have after death that I don't already possess in this life. I shall see God, true; but as far as being in His presence, I am totally there here on earth.[36]

Your darkest hour will be like noon

In his presence here and now, within his community of prayer, in not judging within an unreserved sharing of love, my being is then in Jesus and he in me; I am in Jesus and he in my being.[37] That is the kingdom of our *Abba* Father which even now reigns in this world[38] as we pray for its coming. Having this hope for what I long for but cannot yet see, I am able to await it in persevering confidence,[39] my ears hearing, my eyes seeing, my ways changing, within the action of Jesus.[40]

> Then your light will blaze out like the dawn
> and your wound would be quickly healed over.
> Saving justice for you will go ahead
> and Yahweh's glory come behind you.
> Then you will cry for help and Yahweh will
>   answer;
> you will call and he will say, 'I am here.'
> If you do away with the yoke,
> the clenched fist and malicious words,
> if you deprive yourself for the hungry
> and satisfy the needs of the afflicted,
> your light will rise in the darkness
> and your darkest hour will be like noon.[41]

'Your darkest hour will be like noon.' Why have so many Christians so often been so full of fear? Is it because we have not listened to Jesus with ears opened by him? In his darkest hour the Good Thief, the lawless bandit who had probably cruelly murdered and so been condemned, had but to recognize Jesus in nine words. Then Jesus said eight words: 'Today you will be with me in paradise.'[42] In those words there is no judgement, but only the certain promise of salvation, the full light of noon.

Even the torturers, the baiters of others on grounds of race, belief or birth, have but to say one word that all may be undone — and All done.

Mary of Magdala was weeping, suffering outside the empty Tomb, having lost all that she loved. Jesus called her by name. She replied to him with but one word — *Rabbuni.*

Love is one word. Love is repaid by love alone. The Thirsting One meets his one, loving into the oneness of Love.

Lifted up on the cross, Jesus says to each one of us, 'I am thirsty.' [43] Love seeks and thirsts for each our little love that it may be cast into the furnace of Love to be made fiery, molten, like precious gold:

> See, then, all that Jesus lays claim to from us; He has no need of our works but only of our love, for the same God who declares He has no need to tell us when He is hungry[44] did not fear to beg for a little water from the Samaritan women. He was thirsty. But when He said: *Give me to drink,*[45] it was the love of His poor creature the Creator of the universe was seeking. He was thirsty for love. I feel it more than ever before, Jesus is parched, for He meets only the ungrateful and indifferent among His disciples in the world, and among His own disciples, alas, He finds few hearts who surrender to Him without reservations, who understand the real tenderness of His infinite Love.[46]

The *Catechism of the Catholic Church* explores this aspect of prayer further:

The wonder of prayer is revealed beside the
well where we come seeking water: there,
Christ comes to meet every human being. It is
he who first seeks us and asks us for a drink.
Jesus thirsts; his asking arises from the depths
of God's desire for us. Prayer is the encounter
of God's thirst with ours. God thirsts that we
may thirst for him.[47]

Jesus as spiritual director

In her encounter with the divine tenderness in
prayer, in seeking to slake the divine thirst, Thérèse
teaches a reliance on the inspiration of Scripture, and
expresses a deep sense of the direct guidance given by
Jesus within her:

If I open a book composed by a spiritual
author (even the most beautiful, the most
touching book), I feel my heart contract
immediately and I read without understanding, so to speak. Or if I do understand, my
mind comes to a standstill without the capacity of meditating. In this helplessness, Holy
Scripture and the *Imitation* come to my aid; in
them I find a solid and very pure nourishment.
But it is especially the Gospels which sustain
me during my hours of prayer, for in them I
find what is necessary for my poor little soul. I
am constantly discovering in them new lights,

hidden and mysterious meanings. I understand and I know from experience that *the
Kingdom of God is within you.*[48] Jesus has no need
of books or teachers to instruct souls; He
teaches without the noise of words. Never
have I heard Him speak, but I feel that He is
within me at each moment; He is guiding and
inspiring me with what I must say and do.[49]

Thérèse does not teach any system of prayer, any set
way, except the disposition of the open, vulnerable
heart in which she knew that Jesus himself was her
spiritual guide, her director:

I believe it is Jesus Himself hidden in the
depths of my poor little heart: He is giving me
the grace of acting within me, making me
think of all He desires me to do at the present
moment.[50]

Moving us from what is so easily seen as the dusty
duty of prayer, she opens to us the delights of being
close to Jesus: 'Jesus, O Jesus, if the *desire* of loving You
is so delightful, what will it be to possess and enjoy this
Love?' Notice, the *desire* is sufficient. We can only *desire
to desire*: Jesus, having awakened that desire to desire,
then does everything according to his loving will. The
more weak and little we are in this desire the better for
its free action in us. Therefore Thérèse invites us to
take Jesus himself as our spiritual director:

I feel that if You found a soul weaker and littler than mine, which is impossible, You would be pleased to grant it still greater favours, provided it abandoned itself with total confidence to Your Infinite Mercy. But why do I desire to communicate Your secrets of Love, O Jesus, for was it not You alone who taught them to me, and can You not reveal them to others? Yes, I know it, and I beg You to do it. I beg You to cast Your Divine Glance upon a great number of *little* souls. I beg You to choose a legion of *little* Victims worthy of Your Love![51]

Thérèse's religious vocation in Carmel was that of a life immersed in prayer. The great teacher of the life of prayer in the Carmelite tradition was Teresa of Avila, who had written with deep wisdom and at great length about the path of the soul through the series of stages in achieving union with God. Her work was buttressed by that of her contemporary, John of the Cross, the man of tender love teaching others to love tenderly. Thérèse was, of course, well versed in these spiritual giants. While retaining their sharp focus on the paramouncy of love, she was led on her path of prayer by Jesus for a specific, and for us in the world, a crucial purpose—for she did nothing that could not be imitated by other 'ordinary' people involved in the many different avenues of life outside any monastery wall.

The unification of thought and action

It was not a question of patronizingly concocting a way for those who could not follow a 'professional' way of prayer. She had every firm intention of avoiding any judgement and of flying straight into the arms of Jesus. So her simple prayer in the little way of love fully served her, as it can serve us. In that simplicity and attentiveness on our part, Jesus himself will teach each one how he wishes him or her to be with him in prayer. In Jesus we are free. Thérèse loved to quote Jesus' saying that in his Father's mansion there are many rooms.

Thérèse takes Jesus at his word: 'Anyone who loves me will keep my word, and my Father will love him and we will come to him and make a home in him . . . you may ask for whatever you please and you will get it.'[52] Going directly to the Scriptures, taking Jesus' words at their true value, she opts for the way of the little one and asks Jesus to do as he promised and *live and act in her*. He carries his little one in his arms. All our thought and action therefore becomes unified in a prayer lived out through all our life and all our concerns and responsibilities, and through our worries and pains. Love is unifying because it is one. All becomes knitted together so that, continually in Jesus' presence, prayer is not just some time set aside from our activity but extends through that activity and conditions it. We can hold an inner quietness and calmness in this continuous reception of the Love living in us. It becomes a continuous loving communion . . . 'it is no longer I, but Christ living in me.'[53]

Paul hints at this way of receptivity to love when he advises us to live quietly[54]—to seek our quiet, to become less dependent on what happens round us, to allow quietness to draw us. This is itself very healing in disturbance and stress. We do not need to go to the mystical Eastern religions to learn escape from turbulence. We can better understand our own traditions and explore them for the insights already present to us:

> My child, do not take on a great amount of business; if you multiply your interests, you are bound to suffer for it; hurry as fast as you can, yet you will never arrive, nor will you escape by running away. Some people work very hard at top speed, only to find themselves falling further behind.
>
> Or there is the slow kind of person, needing help, poor in possessions and rich in poverty; and the Lord turns a favourable eye on him, lifts him out of his wretched condition, and enables him to hold his head high, thus causing general astonishment.[55]

Making room for the inner life

How often do we need to do the things we do? Is there a discernment we can bring to bear to allow more room for ourselves and for Emmanuel 'God-with-us'? Jesus told us to go to our inner room and close the door.[56] He was teaching us to withdraw, to be hidden. That inner room, in a crowded busy home, may at times be the bottom of the garden, in a tool shed, or in the local park as we walk alone.

Thérèse was known to walk quietly past groups of nuns busily talking about matters which were superfluous and inconsequential — or, even if consequential, which need not concern her. This did not stop her from being the life and soul of recreation when the nuns were gathered to relax. We can also keep in mind that our possessions should not possess us, but be under our domain, used for meeting our needs and of those dependent on us, but always used with discrimination and due priority. We can be poor in spirit while having possessions. We *can* be rich in spirit while in want. Then space can open up so that we can 'make time to attend to your inner life, and frequently think over the benefits God has given you.'[57] We can live quietly, and so listen and see with veracity. Thérèse tells us that if we take time to sit and listen—and that can be done in many places, like the corner of a crowded commuter train—we will run in the way of love, we will raise our world of activity and business and distraction:

> For a soul that is burning with love cannot remain inactive. No doubt she will remain at Jesus' feet as did Mary Magdalene, and she will listen to His sweet and burning words. Appearing to do nothing, she will give much more than Martha who torments herself with so many things and wants her sister to imitate her.[58] It is not Martha's works that Jesus finds faults with; His divine Mother submitted

humbly to those works all through her life since she had to prepare the meals of the Holy Family. It is only *the restlessness of His ardent hostess that He willed to correct.*[59]

'Be still and acknowledge that I am God, supreme over nations, supreme over the world.'[60] Can we be simple and still, for example, while offering to Jesus all our concern and worries about the many needs not only of those we know but of all those we do not know? Prayer itself becomes so busy then . . . remember this . . . remember that . . . don't forget that . . . and that other thing I forgot! As though Jesus needs a four-page *aide memoir* put to him to act on! Thérèse's world, for all the enclosure, was much bigger than might seem, involved with the needs of those outside the monastery as well as those inside:

> If I wanted to ask for each soul what each one needed and go into detail about it, the days would not be long enough and I fear I would forget something important. For simple souls there must be no complicated ways; as I am of their number, one morning during my thanksgiving, Jesus gave me a simple means of accomplishing my mission.
>
> He made me understand these words of the Canticle of Canticles: '*Draw me*, we shall run after you in the odour of your ointments.'[61]
>
> O Jesus, it is not even necessary to say: 'When drawing me, draw the souls whom I

love!' This simple statement: *'Draw me'*
suffices; I understand, Lord, that when a soul
allows herself to be captivated by *the odour of
Your ointments,* she cannot run alone, all the
souls she loves are drawn in her train; this is
done without constraint, without effort, it is a
natural consequence of her attraction for You.
Just as a torrent, throwing itself with
impetuosity into the ocean, drags after it
everything it encounters in its passage, in the
same way, O Jesus, the soul who plunges into
the shoreless ocean of Your Love, draws with
her all the treasures she possesses. Lord, You
know it, I have no other treasures than the
souls it has pleased You to unite to mine.[62]

We are being guided again by Thérèse into the way
of simplicity, and into a focusing on Love, avoiding the
babble Jesus warned us against, into what Teresa of
Avila called a conversation between two friends.

Seeking refreshment amid dryness

Thérèse comments upon the dryness which can
affect us all, especially when tired after the work of
many responsibilities; and she proposes a way in that
situation whereby we can pray very simply and quietly:

Sometimes when my mind is in such a great
aridity that it is impossible to draw forth one
single thought to unite me with God, I *very*

slowly recite an 'Our Father' and then the angelic salutation; then these prayers give me great delight; they nourish my soul much more than if I had recited them precipitately a hundred times.[63]

In our human condition, prayer can at times seem painful in itself, with a myriad distractions buzzing round us. Even Teresa of Avila was not above saying, at one stage of her prayer life, 'thankfully, that's done,' when finishing her prayers. However, she also noted that when she had used self-discipline to get herself to prayer, she found greater peace and joy than on some other occasions when she had found it easier to enter prayer. Times of dryness must, it seems, be expected. The texture of daily life varies; humanly we cannot be totally enclosed and cut off from urgent problems, nor always find quietness in adversity. 'But when you see how important it is to you to have His friendship and how much he loves you, you must rise above the pain . . .' wrote Teresa.[64]

The feelings can be flat and discouraged; tiredness besets us after hours of demanding work. Jesus also, being tired by the journey, sat by the well and asked for refreshment.[65] Then is the time in our tiredness for us to sit by his well and simply ask for refreshment, for quiet, trusting, continuing confidence. We need not allow our feelings to swamp us, knowing that our good intent is sufficient for Jesus. We can still gather a straw or two for the fire:

St Teresa [of Avila] says we must feed the fire of love. When we are in darkness, in dryness, there is no *wood* within our reach, but surely we are obliged at least to throw little bits of *straw* on the fire. Jesus is quite powerful enough to keep the fire going by Himself, yet He is glad when we add a little fuel, it is a delicate attention which gives Him pleasure, and then He throws a great deal of wood on the fire; we do not see it but we feel the *strength* of Love's heat.

I have tried it: when I feel *nothing,* when I am *incapable* of praying or practising virtue, then is the moment to look for small occasions, *nothings* that give Jesus more pleasure than the empire of the world, more even than martyrdom generously suffered. For example a smile, a friendly word, when I would much prefer to say nothing at all or look bored, etc.

It is not to make my crown, to gain merits, but to give pleasure to Jesus. When I find no occasions, at least I want to keep telling Him that I love Him, it's not difficult and it keeps the fire going; even if that fire of love were to seem wholly out, I should throw something on it and then Jesus could relight it . . . perhaps you will think that I always act like this. Oh, no! I am not always faithful, but I am never discouraged, I abandon myself in Jesus' arms.[66]

For virtually all her life in religion, Thérèse herself had to endure an aridity which finally in the last eighteen months of her life descended into a desolation of darkness. Exteriorly she remained calm, cheerful and encouraging towards others, while interiorly without consolation, though always peaceful. We must remember when we read of her experience that she was following her path which she had been given by Jesus — we should not make wholesale assumptions about our own given path extrapolated from those of others. Jesus knows our frailty and will provide for each all that is necessary. 'We can never have too much confidence in Jesus — we obtain from Him what we hope for.' The more weak and little the soul, the more will be required. 'The Lord knows our weaknesses, that He is mindful that we are but dust and ashes.'

Thérèse wrote with wry good humour about the spiritual dryness she encountered during her retreat for her Profession as a nun, two and a half years after her entry to the convent:

> It was far from bringing me any consolations since the most absolute aridity and almost total abandonment were my lot. Jesus was sleeping as usual in my little boat; I see very well how rarely souls allow Him to sleep peacefully within them. Jesus is so fatigued with always having to take the initiative and to attend to others that He hastens to take advantage of the repose I offer Him.[67]

Thérèse seems frequently to have fallen asleep at her prayers. She was not dismayed and writes of these experiences with balanced good humour from which we can learn to avoid unnecessary worry and scrupulosity:

> I should be desolate for having slept [for seven years] during my hours of prayer and my thanksgivings after Holy Communion; well, I am not desolate. I remember that *little children* are as pleasing to their parents when they are asleep as when they are wide awake; I remember, too, that when they perform operations, doctors put their patients to sleep. Finally, I remember that: 'The Lord knows our weaknesses, that He is mindful that we are but dust and ashes.'[68]

Prayer is in good will and persistent attempts

For Thérèse prayer was not just a separate time, divided from the world around us. For her, prayer flowed over life so that the love of Jesus and the child's response was always present. Without sentimentality, with good sense and realism, Thérèse taught that a smile when a smile was difficult, a kindness to another when inside was only bleakness, these are prayers, little nothings from our emptiness. We can do no more, yet in the doing of it how much we may have to make ourselves do it! In it all is just that good intent which we maintain, knowing that we do nothing, Jesus does everything. He merely wants our good will, nothing more. He will do the building. Our prayer is in our good will and persistent attempts.

Our love of Jesus does not consist of passing emotions; it is a Spirit-inspired and Spirit-energized commitment, a vulnerable open heart. It is a steady focusing onto Jesus, moment to moment, free from straining and anxiety. We may not even feel love—but we have love in that steady focusing. The author of *The Cloud of Unknowing* discusses the attitude of quiet, trusting equilibrium and cheerful stability such as that lived by Thérèse, which can help us in coping with the movement to and fro between the times of felt love and of those of dryness, or even of a more extensive aridity:

> Do not overstrain yourself emotionally or beyond your strength. Work with eager enjoyment rather than with brute force. Learn to love God with quiet, eager joy, at rest in body as in soul.[69] God is a spirit and whoever would be made one with Him must be in truth and in depth of spirit far removed from any misleading bodily thing. While our longing has any sort of natural element in it (as is the case when we strain and stress ourselves emotionally and spiritually at one and the same moment) it is that much further from God than it would be if there had been greater devotion, and more sober eagerness, purity and spiritual depth.[70] Whoever had the grace to put what I say into practice would have a lovely game spiritually with Him—just as an

earthly father does with his child, hugging and kissing him—and would be glad to have it so.[71]

Thérèse greatly loved and valued the support of community prayer, and this participation in community is essential. Jesus provided the family of his Church as the centre of our devotion to him. Each way of prayer, personal and community, support and sustain each other. Together they realize the praise and love of God, and they are the groundwork and buttresses of the salvation of the world. The daily prayers of the Church provide a framework we can, to one degree or another of simplification, adopt to use to help us in a regular rhythm and pattern of prayer and praise — from which the heart is lifted off to its own spontaneous, free expression to God.

Practice of the presence of God

To practise the little way of love we need to find a way to steadily, quietly and constantly realize Jesus in our heart, mind and soul, always turned to him. Paul said we should pray constantly, without ceasing.[72] St John Chrysostom said no matter where we happen to be, by prayer we can set up an altar to God in our heart. We must remember God more often than we draw breath, said St Gregory of Nazianzus. Jesus as spiritual director will lead each person to that which he wills for them in deepening the loving relationship, the interchange, the conversation between Creator and creature, the sense of his presence and care. In quietness, the right inspirations will be known. In practice the

right opportunities, the seeming 'coincidences' will
happen — the little miracles of the leadings of grace.
'Everything you ask and pray for, believe that you have
it already, and it will be yours.'[73]

It may be helpful to consider briefly one way of the
practice of the Presence of God which has a venerable
history of many centuries to authenticate it. It is a way
that has stood the test in busy, distracted lay life. It is the
Jesus Prayer of the Eastern Orthodox Tradition in the
Church. This Orthodox spiritual treasure has been written about by a Swedish Lutheran, translated by an
Anglican and commended by a Roman Catholic priest.[74]
It is intensely biblical and is simplicity itself. Thérèse
seemingly did not know of it, but in fact her perpetual
disposition of heart and mind shows the presence in her
of the same well of inspiration as is drawn from by the
tradition of the Jesus Prayer. For the prayer is the same
as that of the blind beggar outside Jericho,[75] and of the
Canaanite women with a deranged daughter in the dis-
trict of Tyre and Sidon,[76] and of the ten diseased men
who called upon Jesus for pity on the way from Samaria
to Galilee.[77] The prayer is of dependency and inability:

Lord Jesus Christ, Son of God, have mercy on me a sinner.

We should understand the plea for mercy *without*
any judgmental, stern connotation, but in the sense of
its true meaning as a plea for the *tender loving-kindness* of
the eternal Love. Jesus — and with him is the one
indivisible community of Love of the Blessed
Trinity — in his love thirsts for each of us. The Jesus
prayer is our desire to assent to that Love.

The name 'Jesus' contains all: God and man and the whole economy of creation and salvation. To pray 'Jesus' is to invoke him and to call him within us. His name is the only one that contains the presence it signifies. Jesus is the Risen One, and whoever invokes the name of Jesus is welcoming the Son of God who loved him and who gave himself up for him.[78]

It is the prayer of the little, utterly needful one turning to the Parent and expecting all in All. It is a prayer for the completion of the entire will of God, and for his kingdom. It is the prayer of vulnerable openness and expectation. 'You shelter them, they rejoice in you, those who love your name . . . you surround them with favour as with a shield.'[79]

The invocation of the holy name of Jesus is the simplest way of praying always. When the holy name is repeated often by a humbly attentive heart, the prayer is not lost by heaping up empty phrases, but holds fast to the Word and 'brings forth fruit by patience.'[80] This prayer is possible 'at all times' because it is not one occupation among others but the only occupation: that of loving God, which animates and transfigures every action in Christ Jesus.[81]

The prayer may be silently said slowly, rhythmically and repeatedly so many times that it enters the heart of our being and the echo remains in the mind always.

'Nobody is able to say "Jesus is Lord," except in the Holy Spirit.'[82] The prayer may be conveniently shortened, but the Holy Name and the plea remain. As we pray to Jesus it is the Holy Spirit who draws us, to the Father, into his kingdom.

Thérèse is the saint of involvement—the movement outwards from subjectivity to community and participation. She shows us that prayer is not a closing in on oneself but an opening out onto life and the changing of life. Prayer is the community of the saints in action. Prayer is glorification — our glorification of God; and his glorification, transformation of us into his glory. When Jesus is called upon, he comes, and there is no spiritual darkness; only his light which is so infinite that for now he mercifully makes it the darkness of blind trusting faith in which he may lead silently and securely. In persistence in the simple yearning, the aspiration, the raising of the heart and in simple glances towards heaven, I learn the words, the Word, of Love in which dry duty becomes desire and desire is fulfilled by Love; for prayer 'is something great, supernatural, which expands my soul and unites me to Jesus.'

The little child says very simply to God
what the child wishes to say;
and is persistent in raising the heart
and simple glances towards Heaven
in a cry of love and gratitude
in the midst of trial as well as in joy.
The child never grows weary of praying,
with a confidence which works miracles,
because everything that it asks of its Father
in Jesus' Name will be granted.

Chapter 6

Daily practice of the little way of love

'No one lights a lamp and puts it under a bushel basket, but upon the lampstand, so as to give light to all in the house'. . . Love must not consist in feelings but in works.
St Thérèse, *Story of a Soul*, Ch. X, p. 220 & 222

In perplexity, Ignatius sat on his bed in an upper room of his family's castle in northern Spain. He was reading. He had the only books available to him during his protracted convalescence after a cannon ball had smashed his leg in the French siege of a fortress at Pamplona which he had helped to defend. Ignatius puzzled over the direction his life should now take; a crippled soldier would not be wanted. Until that point in time he had filled his head with the knightly romance literature of the day and could, he tells us in his autobiography, spend hours on end imagining the heroic feats he would perform to serve a distinguished and beautiful lady. On returning home after bravery in battle — in which others had thought it more wise to surrender but Ignatius had insisted on resistance rather than dishonour—he had asked for some of his beloved tales of chivalry and knightly deeds.

Disappointed, Ignatius had to make do with the only two books available: some legends of the saints and a life of Jesus. But these two books had a fundamental and revolutionary effect upon Ignatius. From fantasies of earthly love, Ignatius focused upon the reality of heavenly love. He was a man formed in the military virtues of gallantry, and supportive friendship and loyalty, particularly needed in the relatively small, close-knit fighting formations of those days. He determined to have Jesus for his friend. He decided to become a soldier for Christ. He would do gallant deeds for Jesus, without counting the cost. He set out to join the army of the Lord. Ignatius had solved his perplexity—or rather, God had resolved it in his grace and leadings.

We are indebted to St Ignatius of Loyola (1491-1556) for his faithfulness to his vocation and his eventual founding of the Society of Jesus which, renowned for scholarship and self-giving, grew rapidly and undertook a major role in the reform of the post-medieval Church.

So often, as soon as there is in us a conviction that God loves, *really* loves and calls, there follows a generous-minded impulsive response into an activism which, even though we know we cannot earn his love, implies that we should in some way justify that priceless love. It is an impulse of generosity but it is creature-led, and so, misled. 'What house could you build me, what place for me to rest, when all these things were made by me and all belong to me? But my eyes are drawn to the person of humbled and contrite spirit' declares Yahweh.[1] Coming from a thoughtful and fruitful spiritual retreat, one of Thérèse's novices told her of her re-fired fervour, filled with great resolutions. But Thérèse advised the novice to be careful, since hell seems to be let loose against such a renewed person to make him or her fall during the first bold steps, so as to discourage and dismay, and make them say: How can I keep my resolutions, if I have fallen so soon? 'So, each time,' said Thérèse, 'they are successful, you must get up again without surprise, and humbly say to Jesus: "They may have knocked me down but I am not beaten. Here I am, standing again and ready to go on fighting for love of You." Then Jesus will be moved by your goodwill, and will Himself be your strength.' To the same novice Thérèse commented, 'If God wants you to be as weak and powerless as a child . . . resign yourself, then, to stumbling at every step, to falling even. *Love your powerlessness,* and your soul will benefit more from it than if, aided by grace, you were to behave with enthusiastic heroism and fill your soul with self-satisfaction and pride.'[2]

Whoever goes too quickly stumbles

Ignatius was wise. 'Where knowledge is wanting, zeal is not good; whoever goes too quickly stumbles.'[3] On reading the lives of Jesus and of his saints while convalescent, he also had been fired with an impulsive desire to copy them, to emulate their heroic deeds. But, to his and our benefit, while retaining his generosity of heart he did not act impulsively. Dedicating his weapons and armour to God, taking up the cross of Jesus—he waited. From the heroic impulses born of the new conviction and commitment, he resolved on a period of quiet waiting and listening. Like the child Samuel in the sanctuary, he became still and expectant, attentive to God. 'Speak, Yahweh, for your servant is listening.'[4] He prayerfully discerned God's will for him.

'Be still and acknowledge that I am God.'[5]

'And after the fire, a light murmuring sound. And when Elijah heard this, he covered his face.'[6]

When God speaks to his child who is selflessly seeking him, he speaks quietly and intimately. The closer the child comes to God, the simpler does he or she become, and the quieter and closer the voice.

St Augustine of Hippo, whose resolution of turmoil in the garden we have already noted, sat with pen in hand pondering God's actions. 'We open our hearts to You,' he wrote, 'so that You may free us wholly, as You have already begun to do. Then we shall no longer be miserable in ourselves, but will find our true happiness in You.' Augustine welcomed his spiritual neediness and poverty amid his desire to serve the Lord, and asked of him: *first give me what I may offer You . . .* for if You are not there to hear us even in our deepest plight, what is to become of us?' He asked of God through Jesus, 'whom You sent to find us when we were not looking for You, and You sent him to find us so that we should look for You.'[7]

Augustine teaches that it is our hearts which are opened to receive Jesus who comes to free us from the misery of ourselves and take us into true happiness with God. All the writer's language is framed on the basis that this is done *to* and *for* us. His pen traces the poverty and patience in which we are to await Jesus and his action in us in which he calls us to freedom,[8] the freedom of the law of Love in the practice of which our every undertaking will be blessed.[9]

'In God,' said Mother Teresa of Calcutta, 'I find two things admirable: His goodness and His humility. His love and His humility are striking. God is truly humble; He comes down to us and uses instruments as weak and imperfect as we are. He deigns to work through us. Is that not marvellous?' We are not channels, we are instruments. Channels give nothing of their own, they just let the water run through them. In our actions we are instruments in God's hands. 'God writes through us and, however imperfect instruments we may be, He writes beautifully.'[10]

'Creatures are *means,* instruments He uses, but it is Jesus' hand that *governs all.* In *everything* you must see only Him,' wrote Thérèse.[11]

God acts first on his own initiative

The *Catechism of the Catholic Church* describes this creative action of God through our free choice of collaboration with him, under the guidance and power of the Holy Spirit:

Between God and us there is an immeasurable inequality, for we have received everything from him, our Creator. The merit of man before God in the Christian life arises from the fact that *God has freely chosen to associate man with the work of his grace.* The fatherly action of God is first on his own initiative, and then follows *man's free acting through his collaboration,* so that the merit of good works is to be attributed in the first place to the grace of God, then to the faithful. Man's merit, moreover, itself is due to God, for his *good actions proceed in Christ, from the predispositions and assistance given by the Holy Spirit.*[12]

'Jesus does *everything,* I do *nothing,*' Thérèse the vigorous missionary wrote. 'In the evening of this life I shall appear before You with *empty hands,* for I do not ask You, Lord, to count my works . . . I wish then to be clothed in your own justice and to receive from Your Love the eternal possession of Yourself.'[13]

The great worker Augustine prayed, 'Lord, perfect *Your work* in me.' He did *not* pray, Lord perfect *my work* in You!

Our Creator God, entirely and utterly of his own love for each of us, wills to draw us into and associate us with his creative work. The *Catechism* describes that happy time — before the event of the Fall when humanity chose to be like a god but without God — that happy time in which the Creator had shown the extent of his familiar trust and sharing:

The sign of man's familiarity with God is that God places him in the garden [14]. There he lives 'to till it and keep it.' Work is not yet a burden,[15] but rather the *collaboration* of man and woman with God *in perfecting the visible creation.*[16]

Despite the loss of that Garden, even in our fallen state now:

To human beings God even gives the power of freely sharing in his providence by entrusting them with the responsibility of 'subduing' the earth and having dominion over it.[17] They then fully become *God's fellow workers and co-workers*[18] for his kingdom.[19]

God, in humility, takes the initiative in proposing to us. After our free consent is given, as a tenderly supportive parent he holds us up and assists us, giving us the gifts of grace necessary to serve him who in his perfection has no need; he then humbly shares with us the glory and the merit, the crown, which strictly are his. The Father wills, creates and graces, the Son saves, frees and endows, the Spirit facilitates, sustains, and leads. The collaborating, receptive, endowed creature returns all to God with praise and thanksgiving. As the Blessed Trinity, the one indivisible community of Love, calls each, each is called into one loving community to exercise the gratuitous gifts of service bestowed by God in his work of grace to gather all into his kingdom.

To pray for light

By this we are freed as children of God. We are freed of our own inward-regarding compulsions and slavery; and the pain of the need to prove ourselves. We can act with a graced freedom, free of self-sterilization — whenever Thérèse noticed a tendency in any of her novices to become closed in on themselves, she fought it vigorously, saying: 'To become introverted is to sterilize the soul.' Of course we can propose to Jesus as we vigorously go about his purpose; but 'have you taken care to commend what you are about to God? It is very important to renew one's spirit of faith on these occasions, and to pray for light,' she told one of her novices she found hurrying to a meeting, 'If you haven't done that, you are wasting your time.'[20]

We are freed into poverty in an utter dependency on a source which calls, leads, provides, and gathers. We are called to receive — we are called to receptivity. We are called to burn with love given to us; we are not called to spontaneous combustion. False pride will always tempt us to works which attract us and which must — mustn't they? — be meritorious! On the contrary, we are called to receptivity and creativity, in Jesus. We have ideas, but Jesus has invigorating and arousing inspiration.

'The chief cause of your sufferings and troubles is that you look at things too much from an earthly point of view, and not enough from a supernatural viewpoint. You seek your own satisfaction in things to too great an extent. But you won't find any happiness until you stop looking for it,' Thérèse advised a novice.[21]

We return to Ignatius. On his recovery from his leg injury (though still limping) he moved to Manresa, near the abbey at Montserrat in eastern Spain, and spent a year waiting on God and writing the first draft of his *Spiritual Exercises*. This time of prayer and recollection away from the world was a period of his formation for the work to come. But he was, in truth, already at work in his patient seeking of God's will for him, the discernment of the unique mission gifted to him as a co-worker of Jesus. Beset in his conversion, his re-birth, by impelling and immense desires in the service of God, he nevertheless wanted to discern what God willed of him and to receive the courage to carry it out.

The word *discernment* is rooted in the Latin for *sifting*; that is, sieving. God says:

'For look, I shall give the command
and shall shake out the House of Israel among
    all nations
as a sieve is shaken out . . .'[22]

In his *Spiritual Exercises*,[23] Ignatius explains that:

Going for long or short walks and running are physical exercises; so we give the name of spiritual exercises to any process which makes the soul . . . discover how God wills it to regulate its life; in the search for the divine will, the Creator and Lord should be left to deal Himself with the soul that belongs to Him, receiving it into His love and to a life of praise, *fitting it for that form of service which is best for it* in the time to come.

From the heart of his own experience of God's sifting of him, Ignatius developed his ideas on a process of discernment from within the desolations and consolations he experienced during his prayerful search for God's will for him, and he wrote his conclusions regarding their import and consequences. During the rest of his life he periodically revised his work, enabling the final edition of the *Spiritual Exercises* to be published after his death, with an effect which is worldwide, among all nations.

Consolations and desolations

A consolation, or comfort, in Ignatius's teaching, is any interior movement of the affections which causes a glow of love for God, an increase in faith, hope and love centred on God, bringing peace and tranquillity in him. A desolation, or distress, is the opposite state; one of disquiet, restlessness, disturbance, temptation, apathy and so on, which reduce faith, hope and love, tending to a lessening awareness of God. Ignatius stipulates that decisions on our purposes should be taken from and within periods of consolation; while such decisions should not be altered during periods of desolation but instead we should resort to prayer and good practices. This way of discernment provides, as it were, a spiritual compass bearing. Direction should be established when we are aware of openness and closeness to God, since then the leadings of the Holy Spirit are clear to us; but no change in such good directions should be made when we are distressed. In those disturbed times we should be patient and stable, sure of the coming comfort, and knowing that God is still close but is then showing us our need to learn and grow in trust in him—or, he is showing us what it is like when we try to go our own way.

The context of these interior states is crucial. The person who is living in a way which excludes God will be influenced by a destructive spirit towards illusory, passing pleasures which leave behind them only unrest and dissatisfaction; but the Holy Spirit will work on the conscience of such a person to bring them to healing sadness and comforting remorse. The contrary movements will apply to the person making efforts to follow the Holy Spirit. The Spirit will encourage and console, even in the most disturbing circumstances being endured by that person; while a destructive spirit will seek to cause sad uncertainty and distressing doubt.

In periods of comforting consolation by the Holy Spirit, we should take strength for the testing times ahead. We should at all times maintain calm faith in God and his complete care and loving support, despite any periodical disturbance. The Lord's Prayer contains a relevant clause which Jesus gave us with which to ask for support — *lead us not into temptation (the test), but deliver us from evil.* Mother Julian advises us:

The wisest thing is to obey the will and counsel of our greatest, our supreme friend, Jesus. It is Jesus' will and he counsels us to stick with him and hold tightly to him — always, no matter what state we are in. Whether we are filthy or clean, we are always the same to him in his love; whether for good or for bad, he never wants us to run away from him.[24]

Those moving away from God *need* to be distressed to stir them back to him:

We are not able to receive the gentle strength of the Holy Spirit until we have experienced this fear of pain, of physical death and of spiritual enemies. It is this fear which prompts us to seek the strength and mercy of God, and thus this fear helps us by leading us to God and enabling us to come to repentance under the blessed touch of the Holy Spirit.[25]

The one who is sincerely seeking God, and his will, may endure the test remaining absolutely confident in him, resolutely turned to him, in a growth of trusting dependency and utter reliance on him. This is why this interruption of sensed comfort happens, and it can be a very fruitful period, even borne for Jesus with peace and an inner joy! It can be dedicated to the salvation of an unknown person living without God, to bring another back to him:

When we start to hate sin and amend our ways according to the laws of Holy Church we find we are harbouring a fear that holds us back. It comes when we look at ourselves and our past sins. When we see all this we are so sorry and depressed that we are almost beside ourselves. Sometimes we call this fear humility, but that is an error. God wants us to turn to love for our confidence and encouragement: it is love which makes strength and wisdom accessible to us. Just as God in his kindness forgives us our sin the moment we repent, so he wishes us ourselves to forgive our sin of unreasonable depression and doubting fear.[26]

The purpose of discernment

The purpose of this discussion of Ignatius's method of discernment is summed up in an excellent guide by David Lonsdale S.J., which provides much more detail than is possible in the present chapter:

> The process of discernment of spirits therefore is one of *looking at* and *sifting* our present and past experience, taking note especially of the events, people and situations that are associated with or evoke the moods and feelings of consolation and desolation. When we look at the present and immediate future in this way the aim of discernment is to help us to

make choices which encourage and build on the events and situations that are associated with consolation. The reason behind this is that it is characteristic of the Spirit of God to produce consolation, to work for that which is life-giving, creative, joyful, peaceful and so on — the fruits of the Spirit. So our past experiences of consolation show us times when the Spirit has been at work in our lives. And in the present and future our path of truth and growth in discipleship is to choose those ways of being, those courses of action that bring consolation, *for that is to respond to the Spirit's leadings.*[27]

The use of discernment in the manner taught by Ignatius is very helpful in both understanding any initial call by God to a vocation or particular service, and in understanding the movements of feelings and moods while following a deeper spiritual life. Although this process is ostensibly inward-looking, its intention is that one becomes more sensitively tuned to God in an outward movement in loving service. The inward movement is therefore purposeful and not self-regarding, producing its own inbuilt checks and balances.

While Thérèse does not give any extended teaching on discernment as such, she had a gift of understanding spiritual states which amazed even herself at times. Her novices, she tells us, often said to her that she had an answer for everything, having had sound relevant spiritual advice from her, even on personal spiritual matters which they had not confided to her. She commented that she felt that God was very close and that, without realizing it, she had 'spoken words, as does a child, which came not from me but from Him.' As we saw earlier, she regarded Jesus as her spiritual director. Depending upon this inner unheard voice, she had therefore to be very attentive to her interior movements of feelings and attitudes, while avoiding any self-centredness or morbidity. She firmly opposed any morbid tendency in herself and her novices with outwardly directed works of love and service. Nevertheless her inner attentiveness was maintained. She clearly discerned the differences between inner states, so that she constantly expressed her feelings of joy and peace even when enduring a thickening spiritual darkness. Her discernment in any situation was evidently based upon an assessment of the increased or decreased ability to give energy and commitment to exterior duties and service — in other words, the capacity to reach more and more out in love to others. 'Anyone who loves his brother remains in light and there is in him nothing to make him fall away.'[28] It is a healthy, sound extrovert approach to spiritual growth. 'You will be able to tell them by their fruits.'[29]

The rich gifts given in our dependency

The daily practice of the little way of love is an ever deeper exploration of our poverty and incapacity

within love; a thoughtful, but not introverted, sifting of
our inner experiences and emotions; and a discerning
use of the rich gifts of praise and service which we
receive in complete dependency — led by the Holy
Spirit, in Jesus, in a loving movement always outwards
from the self.

Our Father knows what I need even before I call on
him.[30] My only need always is him. I need his gift of
discernment to see his presence and to discover the act
of creation into which he invites me *now*. For the freed
slave the past does not exist, because it has been placed,
baptized, into the Tomb and Death of Jesus. In being
forgiven, it is forgotten:

> The past will not be remembered
> and will come no more to mind.
> Rather be joyful, be glad for ever at what I am
>   creating,
> for look, I am creating Jerusalem to be 'Joy.'[31]

The future is solely the concern of God, who in his
providence raises me in the resurrection of Jesus. The
now is rich from the prayerful waiting on the Lord and
in his facilitating and leading in my creative activity in
a movement from enclosed human pain into Christ and
his sufferings; a movement of release from encircled
self to the need of others; I am made 'like a
well-watered garden, sorrowing no more, mourning
changed into gladness, comforted, given joy after
troubles.'[32]

Creativity compared with activity

Activity and creativity are not necessarily the same. Activity arises all too often from agitation. Such activity is impetuous. It arises from the creature and is therefore fractured and in conflict with itself; that is, contradictory and changing. It does not relate things or needs in due order; it is too often disorderly. The world, in its fractured relationship with God, is full of activity, which causes us to feel distressed, tired, frustrated, unsatisfied. It causes pain and does not allay suffering. It puts us under the dominion of pain, despite our efforts to find ways to prevent pain. An evening's ordinary television fare shows the truth of this, let alone all the other activities to which the world invites us so disarmingly — so many the fruit of the tree of knowledge of good and evil. Thérèse and Ignatius teach us to re-awaken to that attentive sensitivity to God and to his immediacy which was so damaged by the Fall, trapping us into pride and self-dependence; and into distance from God from whom we pull away so childishly with the urge of 'let *me* do it!'

Creativity is calming and consoling, from its fruitfulness in integration with Jesus and his Spirit and the consequent healing it brings. The Holy Spirit is the Spirit of Comfort. He brings us to recollection, that peace which Jesus promised us as his disciples. In his integrating power within the dominion of the creativity and love of God, pain and suffering do not cease to be, but they are subdued, they are placed under our dominion amid a quiet assurance and joy in Jesus. Jesus promised that we would, remaining in him, have all the fruitfulness of heaven; so with confidence in him we join with the angels and the Church militant and vigorous, to battle with this earth to turn it round to God; where it was before Adam fell. 'Remain in me, as I in you . . . I call you friends . . . you may ask for whatever you please . . . you will be sorrowful but your sorrow will turn to joy . . . that joy no one shall take from you . . . In the world you will have hardship, but be courageous, I have conquered the world.'[33]

We are called back to prayer — but since prayer should overflow all our life and action, we are, to put it more specifically, called at all times to attend upon his small Voice in a living, loving relationship. Inwardly quiet and gathered and centred on him, outwardly calm and recollected, we hear him through his world and in our work in his world, responsive and faithful to the leadings of the Holy Spirit. With a simple heart, the happenings, the co-incidences happen. A sensitivity is needed which the Spirit provides in the gifts of conscience and discernment; what is truthful and fortifying and reassuring is from the love of Jesus and is born of the Spirit; what is a lie against the love of Jesus is not of the Spirit. Jesus and the Spirit are one in the Father. Then from an attentive attitude and discerning receptivity will flow fruitful creativity in God-centred and God-led activity. I am given my vocation.

The movement of love within action and prayer

The constant movement of our love between prayer and action is a communion. In the penetration of love into our prayer and action we remain in constant communion with Jesus. Our little trinity of love, prayer, action, in communion, echoes the great Holy Trinity of the abiding Essence of God, the indwelling Action of God and the binding Love of God, in one communion.

In the movement of our love within prayer and action we are each given our vocation. Each child of God has a vocation, the particular creativity into which each is called in communion.

Thérèse teaches us that in this communion with Jesus our desires should be immoderate. She led the way for us and set us an example:

> I understood that love comprised all vocations, that love was everything, that it embraced all times and places . . . in a word, that it was eternal! I cried out: O Jesus, my Love . . . my vocation, at last I have found it . . . *my vocation is Love!*[34]

Thérèse meant this immoderate desire quite literally. In her Act of Oblation to Merciful Love she said, equally inordinately:

> I am certain, then, that You will grant my desires; I know, O my God, that *the more You want to give, the more You make us desire.* I feel in my heart immense desires and it is with confidence I ask You to come and take possession of my soul. I cannot receive Holy Communion as often as I desire, but, Lord, are

You not all-powerful? *Remain in me as in a
tabernacle* and never separate Yourself from
Your little victim.[35]

Mother Agnes of Jesus, Thérèse's sister Pauline, was
asked by the tribunal set up in 1911 to investigate the
life and virtues of Thérèse whether this request that
Jesus remain in her as in a tabernacle (where the
Eucharistic Real Presence is reserved in the Catholic
Church, between Masses, for the sick and for
adoration) was meant by Thérèse in a metaphorical
sense or was to be taken literally. Mother Agnes's reply
was that she was certain that the words were meant
literally.[36] Thérèse's utter confidence in Jesus made her
audaciously daring in her requests. When she
considered God's longing and protective love, she had
no doubts about his infinite capacity to satisfy her
infinite desires. She went further and, stating her own
incapability of holiness, she therefore asked *God to be
her holiness himself.* She therefore made an offering,
without reservation and then placed the responsibility
for its fulfilment upon God himself—while continuing
her life of little actions within unlimited love. We may
quail before the extent of the offering she made, but her
logic cannot be denied; and certainly she saw souls
even more little than she (if that were possible, she
commented) as being even more qualified than she to
offer so radically, since they would be the more
endowed by God in their greater need. 'The more You
want to give, the more You make us desire.'

It is from the constant communion, in the Holy
Spirit, with Jesus, that the seamless robe of love in

prayer and action in love is made. *You come to meet those who are happy to act uprightly; keeping your ways reminds them of you.*[37] We cannot make Jesus a part-time conviction, we cannot put Jesus on the sideline, to be referred to intermittently, and still succeed in the little way of love. There has to be a radical re-alignment upon him, and then constancy in him. Then love in prayer is action, and loving action is prayer. Within our incapability within Jesus' omnipotence all action is submitted to Jesus, and through him it is made holy and effective.

All through the 'lens' of Jesus' action

Therefore while Thérèse's desires are confidently unlimited, her actions are those available to her within the warp and web of her daily life. She consequently and paradoxically does not worry that her practical opportunities for action are devoid of dramatic opportunity or effect. All is submitted through the 'lens' of Jesus' action and so the smallest submitted action has the potential of his total salvific action. Thérèse ceases to worry about the size of her actions, and she no longer keeps an accounting system. She does what Jesus places before her *now,* and is content in the desire simply to please Jesus in all she does; and at the same time her heart is filled with infinite desires to serve him through all the vocations he ever calls into being. She has a very acute sense of what the communion of saints, the community of service, is about.

The advantage for Thérèse in this, and it is an advantage we also surely share, is that what is then done is hidden from human eyes and we are then protected from ostentation and pride. It is not that little actions are more efficacious that big ones, for we have given up comparing actions and keeping accounts. It is not that a lot of little actions will measure up to a number of big ones, for we know in any event that we will go back to God in humility with empty hands, for nothing we can do can even exist in comparison with his creativity. What we are to do is what is placed before us *now* by Jesus. Since the lives of most of us are concerned with 'little' things devoid of 'greatness,' our action will be 'little.' In this way a vowed religious, an enclosed contemplative nun, has revealed an ideal concept for lay spirituality and holiness in the world. The smallness and the lack of ostentation in action — its 'hiddenness' — is within our capacity and field of action, amid our unlimited offering and desires. We know that a small object consumed in a furnace will produce products of combustion which will percolate through the entire atmosphere. In Chinese wisdom, the butterfly moves its wings and the effect is felt throughout the universe. John of the Cross tells us that the smallest action done in pure love has power greater than all other works put together.

That surely is the point about the alignment of activity. Outward-flowing love is creative, and boundless love is infinitely creative. Activity in pure, non-self-centred love becomes creativity and so a seamless part of God's robe of creativity. That is surely why Thérèse understood that she does nothing, Jesus does all. The movement of the creature in pure love from self-centre to Jesus-centre, his constant real presence within, makes differentiation impossible. The impulse is Jesus, the action is Jesus, the fruition is Jesus, within the child of Jesus.

God is drawn to my weakness and inability. He is drawn to that good-will which is necessary if I am to be open to his action, and which he enables by his Spirit in me. He accepts the smallest, the least, movement and act of real love on my part. Then, with a love which reaches even to folly, he will act for me, in creative collaboration between the Father and his child, between the Creator and his creature. Then with St John of the Cross I can say: Now I occupy myself and all my energy in his service. Thérèse reaches the pinnacle of her canticle to Love:

> O my God! Most Blessed Trinity, I desire to *Love* You and make You *Loved,* to work for the glory of Holy Church by saving souls on earth and liberating those in purgatory. I desire to accomplish Your will perfectly and to reach the degree of glory You have prepared for me in Your Kingdom. I desire, in a word, to be a saint, but I feel my helplessness and I beg You, O My God, to be Yourself my *Sanctity.* Since You loved me so much as to give me Your Only Son as my Saviour and my Spouse, the infinite treasures of His merits are mine. I offer them to You with gladness, begging You to look

upon me only in the Face of Jesus and in His
heart burning with *Love*.[38]

We are not alone

If such spiritual ambition seems not to entirely relate
to the scale of the daily practice of the little way of love
in which there are little actions and endeavours,
Thérèse can again help us to understand, through her
magnificent insight on the community of Love, the
communion of saints which has already been quoted
but is of such importance it can be meditated upon
many times. We are not alone:

> Sister Marie of the Eucharist wanted to light
> the candles for a procession; she had no
> matches; however, seeing the little lamp
> which was burning in front of the relics, she
> approached it. Alas, it was half out; there
> remained only a feeble glimmer on its
> blackened wick. She succeeded in lighting her
> candle from it, and with this candle, she
> lighted those of the whole community. It was,
> therefore, the half-extinguished little lamp
> which had produced all these beautiful flames
> which, in their turn, could produce an infinity
> of others and even light the whole universe.
> Nevertheless, it would always be the little
> lamp which would be first cause of all this
> light. How could the beautiful flames boast of
> having produced this fire, when they

themselves were lighted with such a small spark?

It is the same with the communion of saints. Very often, without our knowing it, the graces and lights that we receive are due to a hidden soul, for God wills that the saints communicate grace to each other through prayer with great love, with a love much greater than that of a family, and even the most perfect family on earth. In Heaven we shall not meet with indifferent glances, because all the elect will discover that they owe to each other the graces that merited the crown for them.[39]

Repeatedly, Thérèse, having disposed of the problem of fear of God, stresses that being ourselves we shall fail and fall sometimes, or frequently, and even commit infidelities in our weakness. But if we persist and return to our compass bearing on the frail child on the little way in a daily practice of love, we can draw profit from every happening. Love quickly consumes everything which can be displeasing to Jesus, leaving nothing but the profound peace of humility in the heart. The sadness of failure can be offered, in recognition of our innate dependency. 'When I commit a fault that makes me sad I hasten to say to God: I have merited this feeling of sadness. I'm happy to have this suffering to offer to You.' Not one scrap of the experience need be wasted, and the intention in goodwill is sufficient. 'Give, always give, without being concerned about the results.'[40]

Thérèse, we are told by one of her novices, had a knack of turning all her actions, even the least of them, into acts of love. Sister Marie of the Trinity one day hurt Thérèse's feelings by obstinately refusing to admit some faults. On the way from the discussion, called by the bell to community activity, Sister Marie suddenly felt compunction and whispered her apology to Thérèse. The face of Thérèse was transformed with tenderness as she replied:

> I have never felt so keenly the love with which Jesus receives us when we ask His pardon after offending Him. If a poor little creature of His like me could feel so much love for you when you came back to me, what must God feel when people come back to Him?[41]

Like Ignatius in his pre-conversion chivalric daydreaming, we can imagine our splendid actions in great events — but it is in the little events, and in our reactions in them, that we so easily hit the dust, and miss the moment when the least action done in pure love could have outweighed all other actions done without love. Instead, Thérèse had grasped the moment and filled it with Jesus. 'Without love, all works are nothing,' she taught.[42] She had learned well from St John of the Cross, that *the smallest act of pure love is of more value than all other works put together*[43] — and from her beloved source of inspiration, the *Imitation of Christ:*

A good deed done without love goes for nothing, but if anything is done from love, however small and inconsiderable it may be, every bit of it is counted. God considers what lies behind the deed, and not what is actually done.[44]

Awareness of the presence of God

If we are watching what is happening with discernment, we can receive and understand those insights, such as Thérèse's insight into the endlessly welcoming love of Jesus quoted above, which come to aid us and which Thérèse found often outside the formal, set times of prayer and within the detail of daily activities and concerns. This recollection and discernment in Thérèse was seen and noted by one of her novices who remarked that Thérèse always paused a moment before answering any question put to her, and always arranged things with a view to pleasing God.[45] 'A flood of words is never without fault; whoever controls the lips is wise.'[46] Thérèse did not act on impulse. She reflected and then acted. In that action she was continually aware of Jesus and acted within his love. In that way every moment was given an eternal significance. It is in her recollected prudence that Thérèse shows us the value and practicality of imbuing action with a prayerful attitude, and making prayer action-centred. This is the patient, persistent, daily practice of awareness of the presence of God, the continuous closeness of Jesus; the continual attempt to

surrender into him all that we see and say and hear and
do. This is the recurring recollection of him in the
forgetfulness of self; the finding of the Other in All as
we assist and serve others in all the humble moments of
our day. This spirit is summed up by the *Imitation of
Christ*:

> Give up self, surrender yourself, and you will
> know great peace in your heart. Give your all
> for the one who is all; expect nothing, want
> nothing back; leave yourself with me wholly
> and without regrets, and you will possess me.[47]

'All goods were given me when I no longer sought
them through self-love,' wrote St John of the Cross.[48]
'As long as we love each other God remains in us and
his love comes to perfection in us.'[49]

The smallness of the little way of love enables it to fit
into any and every smallness of our lives. It is a way in
which to take every little straw that we find, to use as
our flimsy fuel for the fire of the love of Jesus which he
will then stoke up in the heart with his immeasurable
fuel. Sister Marie of the Trinity described how anyone
could see that Thérèse never lost sight of the presence
of God and expressed this through the careful attention
which she gave to each small task. 'Who has been
through this test and emerged perfect? He may well be
proud of that! Who has had the chance to sin and has
not sinned? His fortune will be firmly based.'[50] One day
Sister Marie threw on the coverlet of her bed
haphazardly and was reproved by Thérèse for
carelessness, saying that one could hardly be united to

God and do things that way! 'What are you doing in Carmel, if you don't behave spiritually?' she said.[51] This surely is the fidelity in little things of which Jesus speaks as the way to be given big things; especially, surely, if that attention to him in small things is given for another in the daily tasks of home and work. This spirit is reflected in one of John Wesley's sermons in which he said: 'Slovenliness is no part of religion; no text of Scripture condemns neatness of apparel. Certainly this is a duty, not a sin. Cleanliness is indeed next to Godliness.' Thérèse expressed it this way: 'not missing any opportunity of making some small sacrifice, controlling every look and every word, profiting by the least actions and doing them for love.'[52]

This attention to small actions within the daily practice of the little way of love maintains direction in those times, and they may be many, when a felt sense of the Presence is absent. It is then that Ignatius helps us to see that we should keep without change those good resolutions and bearings gained in times of consolation, working patiently and resolutely through times of dryness and even distress. As the *Imitation* says:

> While you live in the flesh, the burden of the flesh will prove a sorrow to you, for it will not let you devote yourself to spiritual thoughts and contemplation of God without interruption. At such times it is best for you to turn to lowlier outward activities, and refresh your soul in good works, confidently waiting

for me to come and visit you and you are freed
from all your anxieties. For I will make you
forget your unhappiness and grant you peace
in your heart.[53]

Love is not in feelings but in works

There is in this the truth of a teaching of Thérèse,
reflecting St John of the Cross, that when our love for
another person is wholly spiritual and based on God
alone, then as it grows the love of God in us grows with
it.[54] We tend to see the situation the other way around,
but Ignatius teaches us to understand that we find God
in the things of our own world and in the activities
within that world, not in some 'spiritualized'
daydreaming about all we would like to do dramatically
if only we could be released from where we are onto a
greater stage. 'Love must not consist in feelings but in
works,' said Thérèse.[55] God is where I am, because he
put me there, and his love is to be found there, however
mundane that place may now appear. But by my
creative activity *here* and *now* in Jesus, *his grandeur will
flame out, like shining from shook foil.*

The strands begin to knit together. In my attempts
to be in a recollected discernment of the presence and
action of Jesus in the detail and passing moments of my
day, in my trying to realize him in my heart through a
quiet echoing of the Name of Jesus, in my seeking to act
outwardly in his love to please and console and give joy
to Jesus, I shall fail and fall. Taking Thérèse's guidance,
I shall get up again. The spirit of destructiveness will

whisper to me and try to discourage me. But I shall hold to the Name of Jesus through the abiding power of the Spirit, and I shall believe his promise of his peace. Then Jesus — seeing me looking always to him from the bottom of the stairway, from the depths, and he always looking to me with the eyes of Love—will come down to me and will take me into his arms. He will enable and carry me in what I myself cannot do and where I myself cannot go unless always in and by his action. From my Good Friday I am taken into his Easter. His cross always leads to and realizes his Resurrection. He wills to share with me all that is his. From my fruitlessness I am pruned into his eternal fruitfulness.

Not one scrap of this experience in this movement, from self-sterility to fruition in Jesus, need be regretted nor lost. For Mother Julian teaches us that even the scars of the wounds of sin we bear will be made glorious in heaven, when:

> We shall see clearly in God the secret things which are now hidden from us. Then none of us will have the slightest urge to say, 'Lord, if it had been like this, then it would have been fine.' Instead we shall all say with one voice; 'We praise You, Lord, because it is like this: all is well. Now we can really see that everything has been done just as You planned it before anything was made. Let us all pray for love. With God working in us, let us thank and trust and enjoy Him.[56]

Sister Marie told Thérèse that she was going to explain the little way of love to all her friends and family and so get them also to offer themselves without reservation to Love. Thérèse was anxious that the little way should not be misunderstood and warned Sister Marie that the little way is not a restful one, full of sweetness and consolation. It is, said Thérèse, quite the opposite. The little way of love is the daily practice of the action of love; and love of its nature is totally a self-giving, an emptying of self to provide to the other. Then we remember that we cannot of ourselves do this, but we can only make the offering of ourselves to Jesus; he then does it for us. For in love we want only to please and console Jesus, cheerfully giving joy to Jesus. *Jesus loves a cheerful giver.*[57]

For we obtain from Jesus as much as we hope for—there is, Thérèse further said, 'only one thing to do here on earth: to cast at Jesus the flowers of *little* sacrifices, to take Him by caresses.'[58]

Jesus is God's Word: the Word is Love—in anyone who keeps his Word, Love will reach perfection.[59] I do nothing, Love does everything in me. Love keeps its Word. I need never doubt nor hesitate. In simplicity and trust I can only offer self-surrender, desire and goodwill.

Acting outwardly in love

In her series of revelations of the love of God, Julian was brought in the seventh to a state in which she did not move but experienced in a short time both extreme consolation, in which nothing on earth could have hurt her, and then to the opposite state of desolation in which she felt all alone, depressed and tired of life. There followed a series of these alternating states of mind. Her purpose in telling of this experience is to assure us that, whether in utter joy or in the depths of despair, God never ceases to care protectively — all states exist in one Love. Her crucial point is that however we feel, the reality of our life is to be found in the joy in him. Events afflict us but our feelings of affliction are not to be held to us, nor centred upon, nor should they mislead us into any misbelief that he loves us less. Indeed, she specifically states that sin is not always the cause of the desolation, and this is a most important and reassuring teaching. We should dwell on the thought.

> God wants us to concentrate with all our might on His comfort: for happiness lasts for ever, while pain will pass and will be reduced to nothing for those who are going to be saved. So it is not God's will that we dwell on the painful feelings, and grieve and mourn over them. He wants us to let go of them quickly, and hold onto His endless joy.[60]

If we centre ourselves outwardly and act outwardly in love, then we cease to centre upon our feelings; we are released from subjectivity and the misery of inwardness. 'For Christ works in us by his mercy, and in grace we yield ourselves to him through the gifts and the power of the Holy Spirit. This work in us makes us

Christ's children, and enables us to live Christian lives.'[61] If we can really accept that, we are released from self-destructive feelings, the work of the spirit of destruction. We can then more certainly discern a way through and from our perplexities, assessing our feelings at their proper value — in the case of hurtful feelings, this value is nil for they will pass away into nothingness. In any state or condition of life, in any disturbance, this must be helpful, even if patience is still called for during the process of release. It is the *facts* of each situation which need to be dealt with concretely, through Jesus in trusting discernment of his will; the hurtful feelings are transitory and the happiness of discovery of fruitful purpose is eternal.

We are taught in the little way of love to learn to see the action of our life as set within Jesus, the Saviour and the Suffering Servant. We then see God concretely at work in all that happens to us as we move even *now* into the victory of the Resurrection, the fruition and peace of Easter. Thérèse's teaching, that the little way is to offer oneself in love in and through Jesus, is applicable within each and every life—and then each is drawn into a renewed perspective of hope, vigour and joy. We do not have to move from where we are to accompany and act in Jesus in his peace in the daily practice of the little way of love, held forever within his arms of Love.

Who ever heard of such a thing,
who ever saw anything like this?
For Yahweh says this:

Look, I am going to send peace
flowing over her like a river,
and like a stream in spate
the glory of the nations.
You will be suckled, carried on her hip
and fondled in her lap.
As a mother comforts her child
so shall I comfort you;
you will be comforted in Jerusalem.
At the sight your heart will rejoice,
and your limbs regain vigour like the grass.[62]

The little child knows that Jesus does not demand great actions
but simply surrender and gratitude,
and that the smallest act of pure love is of more value
than all other works put together.
The child is content to be empty handed,
not asking for its works to be counted,
but doing everything for love,
refusing Jesus nothing,
with the one purpose of pleasing and consoling Jesus,
giving joy to Jesus.

Chapter 7

Epilogue

Since You loved me so much as to give me Your only Son as my Saviour and my Spouse, the infinite treasures of His merits are mine. I offer them to You with gladness, begging You to look upon me only in the Face of Jesus and in His Heart burning with Love.

From St Thérèse's *Act of Oblation to Merciful Love*; *Story of a Soul*, 276

For the Lord Yahweh says this:

Look, I myself shall take care of my flock and look after it. As a shepherd looks after his flock when he is with his scattered sheep, so shall I look after my sheep. I shall rescue them from wherever they have been scattered on the day of clouds and darkness. I myself shall pasture my sheep, I myself shall give them rest—declares the Lord Yahweh I shall look for the lost one, bring back the stray, bandage the injured and make the sick strong. I shall watch over the fat and healthy. I shall be a true shepherd to them.[1]

For I am certain of this:

neither death nor life, nor angels, nor principalities, nothing already in existence and nothing still to come, nor any power, nor the heights nor the depths, nor any created thing whatever, will be able to come between us and the love of God, known to us in Christ Jesus our Lord.[2]

I have sought Your nearness,
with all my heart I called You;
and going out to meet You
I found You
coming to meet me![3]

Then Jesus,
who loves the child even to folly,
does everything for the little one,
for He would not inspire
the longings of the child
unless He wanted to grant them.
Jesus alone
can fulfil immense desires.

Abbreviations of references

SS	*Story of a Soul,* The autobiography of St Thérèse of Lisieux
CL	*Collected Letters of St Thérèse of Lisieux*
LC	*St Thérèse of Lisieux, Her last conversations*
STL	*St Thérèse of Lisieux by those who knew her: testimonies from the process of beatification*
BB	*The Little Way.* Bernard Bro
CCC	*Catechism of the Catholic Church*
CSA	*Confessions of Saint Augustine*
CU	*The Cloud of Unknowing*
ESEH	*Eyes to See, Ears to Hear.* David Lonsdale
FL	*The Four Loves.* C.S. Lewis
HRCH	*How to Read Church History.* Jean Comby with Diarmaid MacCullock
IC	*The Imitation of Christ.* Thomas à Kempis
LW	*Living the Word.* Mother Teresa of Calcutta
RDL	*Revelations of Divine Love.* Mother Julian of Norwich
SADP	*Self-Abandonment to Divine Providence.* Jean-Pierre de Caussade
SESI	*The Spiritual Exercises of Saint Ignatius*
STA	*The Life of Saint Teresa of Avila, by Herself*
VC	*Vatican Council II Documents.* Ed. Austin Flannery
WD	*The Wisdom of the Desert.* Thomas Merton
WDFJ	*We do it for Jesus* — Mother Teresa

Notes

Introduction

1. John 15:14
2. John 16:33
3. John 16:22
4. Luke 18:8
5. Matthew 19:26
6. John 15:16
7. Matthew 5:48

Chapter 2

1. John 3:4
2. John 3:3, 5-7
3. Matthew 18:3-4
4. Matthew 7:24
5. John 18:36
6. Ephesians 4:23-24
7. John 14:6
8. BB 9
9. John 12:24
10. Isaiah 55:1
11. John 12:25
12. Matthew 23:37
13. Matthew 10:39
14. Isaiah 41:24
15. CL 302
16. 1 Corinthians 15:53
17. 2 Corinthians 5:15
18. FL 119
19. John 15:5
20. CL 167
21. Philippians 4:13
22. LC 148
23. CL 302
24. WD 26
25. Luke 22:32
26. LC 140
27. LC 73
28. SADP ch. 2, s.11
29. SADP ch. 2, s.5
30. John 16:21
31. Luke 5:5

32. SS 98
33. SS 101
34. Luke 10:1-17
35. SS 207
36. SS 208 (Proverbs 9:4)
37. SS 208 (Isaiah 66:12-13)
38. SS 208
39. LC 213
40. 2 Corinthians 3:5
41. 2 Corinthians 12:10
42. Psalm 131:2

Chapter 3

1. Luke 6;35
2. Matthew 23:23-24
3. Mark 14:61-64 and Luke 22:66-71
4. Luke 22:37
5. Luke 23:2
6. John 16:30
7. Matthew 5:17
8. Matthew 22:37-40 & Mark 12:29-31
9. John 8:32
10. Galatians 5:1
11. Genesis 3:8
12. Matthew 22:37-38
13. John 13:34
14. LC 45
15. HRCH Vol.2, p.9
16. Romans 3:23-24
17. Romans 5:1
18. Romans 6:13-14
19. SS 188
20. LC 240
21. Romans 4:6-8 and Psalm 32:1-2
22. LC 45
23. LC 43
24. Luke 17:10
25. LC 67
26. IC bk.2, ch.VIII
27. John 15:7, 14

28. RDL from chs. 7, 48, 59
29. LC 74
30. LC 129
31. Luke 11:5-8
32. LC 48
33. 1 John 4:18
34. Tobit 12:7
35. SS 207
36. Romans 8:21
37. Romans 8:23
38. RDL 153
39. 1 Corinthians 12:4-7
40. 1 Corinthians 12:31; 13:1
41. SS 193
42. Luke 18:1-8
43. John 11:43-44
44. Genesis 1:26
45. Genesis 2:18
46. 1 John 4:20
47. Galatians 2:20
48. SS 14
49. VC, Lumen Gentium, 367 (italics my own)
50. Matthew 11:28-30
51. Isaiah 57:14,15,18
52. CL 241
53. CL 320
54. CL 93
55. LC 139
56. SS 259

Chapter 4

1. Isaiah 42:16
2. Exodus 20:19
3. Exodus 33:20
4. Exodus 33:14,17
5. Exodus 33:11
6. Exodus 19:10
7. Hosea, from 2:8-17
8. Isaiah 43:1-3
9. Hosea, from 2:17-22
10. Exodus 13:7
11. LW 36
12. Luke 6:20
13. 1 Corinthians 4:10
14. Mark 15:42-43

15. STL 241
16. STL 245
17. Luke 12:36
18. CL 97
19. Isaiah 38:12-13
20. Matthew 24:43-44
21. Matthew 24:50-51
22. Matthew 24:27-28
23. Matthew 24:42
24. Psalm 77:7-9
25. Exodus 20:5
26. James 4:5-6
27. Luke 12:49
28. SS 187
29. Isaiah 38:14
30. CL 210
31. Isaiah 38:16-17
32. Isaiah 41:24
33. Psalm 72:18
34. Psalm 73: 28
35. Acts 20:35
36. Matthew 12:50
37. John 14:23
38. CL 166
39. Matthew 7:21
40. Matthew 21:28-32
41. CL 253
42. Deuteronomy 1:30-31
43. Matthew 6:33
44. SS 238
45. Proverbs 25:25
46. Matthew 5:3
47. Cf. Matthew 8:20
48. Boosey & Hawkes Music Publishers Ltd 1992
49. Matthew 5:44-45
50. CL 202
51. John 17:17
52. John 18:38
53. Luke 22:28-29
54. Isaiah 63:3,5
55. CL 200
56. Psalm 23:4
57. CL 121
58. SS 213
59. SS 214

60. CL 324
61. SS 180
62. Matthew 5:3
63. Matthew 21:16
64. Ezekiel 36:24-25
65. LC 106
66. Revelations 3:15-16
67. John 20:17
68. John 14:23; CL 200
69. Romans 13:13-14
70. CSA bk. VIII, p.171-178
71. CSA bk. XIII, p. 345
72. CSA bk. X, p.231
73. LC 77
74. STL 249

Chapter 5

1. LC 129
2. Psalm 91:11,14-15
3. CCC para. 2563
4. SS 242
5. Matthew 6:7
6. CU ch. 38
7. 1 Corinthians 12:3
8. John 15:7
9. Ephesians 2:21-22
10. Romans 8:26-27
11. LC 93
12. Ezekiel 36:26-27
13. SS 238
14. Romans 8:2
15. SS 242
16. LC 264
17. STA 62-63
18. LC 71
19. Romans 5:8-10
20. Romans 7:6
21. Romans 8:14-16
22. CU ch. 48
23. LC 57
24. Mark 14:36
25. LC 99-100
26. Romans 8:26-28
27. John 16:23
28. Song of Songs 1:4
29. SS 257
30. SS 258
31. CL 143
32. Matthew 6:9-13
33. Matthew 7:1-2
34. 1 Corinthians 4:3
35. Matthew 21:43
36. LC 45
37. 1 Corinthians 6:17
38. Luke 17:21
39. Romans 8:25
40. Matthew 13:15-16
41. Isaiah 58:8-10
42. Luke 23:43
43. John 19:28
44. Psalm 50:12
45. John 4:7
46. SS 189
47. CCC para. 2560
48. Luke 17:21
49. SS 179
50. SS 165
51. SS 200
52. John 14:23 and 15:7
53. Galatians 2:20
54. 1 Thessalonians 4:11
55. Ecclesiasticus 11:10-13
56. Matthew 6:6
57. IC bk. 2, XX
58. Luke 10:41
59. SS 257
60. Psalm 46:10
61. Song of Songs 1:3
62. SS 254
63. SS 243
64. STA 63
65. John 4:6-7
66. CL 169
67. SS 165
68. Psalm 102:14; SS 165
69. CU ch. 46
70. CU ch. 47
71. CU ch. 46
72. 1 Thessalonians 5:17
73. Mark 11:24
74. See the note on The Jesus Prayer in the bibliography

75. Mark 10:47
76. Matthew 15:22
77. Luke 17:13
78. CCC para. 2666
79. Psalm 5:11-12
80. Luke 8:15
81. CCC para. 2668
82. 1 Corinthians 12:3

Chapter 6

1. Isaiah 66:1-2
2. STL 240 & 250
3. Proverbs 19:2
4. 1 Samuel 3:10
5. Psalm 46:10
6. 1 Kings 19:12-13
7. CSA bk. XI
8. Galatians 5:13
9. James 1:25
10. WDFJ 180-181
11. CL 180
12. CCC para. 2007-8
13. SS 277
14. Genesis 2:8
15. Genesis 2:15; 3:17-19
16. CCC para. 378
17. Genesis 1:26-28
18. 1 Corinthians 3:9;
    1 Thessalonians 3:2; Colossians
    4:11
19. CCC para. 307
20. STL 232
21. STL 232
22. Amos 9:9
23. SESI
24. RDL 155
25. RDL 151
26. RDL 150
27. ESEH 73-74: see note in
    Bibliography

28. 1 John 2:10
29. Matthew 7:16
30. Cf. Matthew 6:8
31. Isaiah 65:17-18
32. Jeremiah 31:12,13
33. John 15:4,15,7; 16:20,22,33
34. SS 194
35. SS 276
36. STL 46
37. Isaiah 64:4
38. SS 276
39. LC 99, 100
40. LC 44
41. STL 235
42. SS 175
43. SS 197
44. IC bk 1, ch. XV
45. STL 260
46. Proverbs 10:19
47. IC bk. 3, ch. XXXVII
48. SS 246
49. 1 John 4:12
50. Ecclesiasticus 31:10-11
51. STL 231
52. STL 122
53. IC bk. 3, ch. LI
54. STL 232
55. SS 222
56. RDL 168
57. Cf. 2 Corinthians 9:7
58. LC 257
59. 1 John 2:5
60. RDL 35
61. RDL 113
62. Isaiah 66:8,12-14

Chapter 7

1. Ezekiel 34:11-12, 15-16
2. Romans 8:38-39
3. 12th century Jewish prayer

Bibliography

Story of a Soul, the autobiography of St Thérèse of Lisieux. Trans. John Clarke O.C.D. from the 1972 publication of the original manuscript as written by St Thérèse. ICS Publications, Washington D.C., 1976

Collected Letters of St Thérèse of Lisieux. Trans. F.J. Sheed. Sheed & Ward, London, 1989

St Thérèse of Lisieux, Her Last Conversations. Trans. John Clarke O.C.D. ICS Publications, Washington D.C., 1977

St Thérèse of Lisieux by those who knew her: testimonies from the process of beatification. Edited and translated by Christopher O'Mahoney. Veritas Publications, Dublin, 1975

Catechism of the Catholic Church. Geoffrey Chapman Publishers, 1994

Confessions of Saint Augustine. Trans. R.S. Pine-Coffin. Penguin Books, 1975

Eyes to See, Ears to Hear — an Introduction to Ignatian Spirituality. David Lonsdale S.J. Darton, Longman and Todd Ltd., 1991

How to Read Church History. Jean Comby with Diarmaid MacCullock. SCM Press, 1989

Living the Word, A New Adventure in prayer involving Scripture, Mother Teresa of Calcutta and You. Compilers: Eileen Egan and Kathleen Egan O.S.B. Fount Paperbacks, HarperCollins, 1991

Revelations of Divine Love. Mother Julian of Norwich. Eds. Halcyon Backhouse with Rhona Pipe. Hodder and Stoughton Ltd., 1992

Self-Abandonment to Divine Providence. Jean-Pierre de Caussade S.J. William Collins Ltd. Fontana Library, 1974

The Cloud of Unknowing. Trans. Clifton Wolters. Penguin Books, 1971

The Four Loves. C.S. Lewis. William Collins Ltd., Fontana Books, 1965

The Imitation of Christ. Thomas à Kempis. Trans. Betty I. Knott. William Collins Ltd., Fount Paperbacks, 1990

The Life of Saint Teresa of Avila, by Herself. Trans. J.M. Cohen. Penguin Books, 1957

The Little Way—the Spirituality of Thérèse of Lisieux. Bernard Bro O.P. Darton Longman & Todd, 1997

The Spiritual Exercises of Saint Ignatius. Trans. Thomas Corbishley S.J. Anthony Clarke Publishers, 1973

The Wisdom of the Desert. Thomas Merton. Sheldon Press, 1975

Vatican Council II, The Conciliar and Post Conciliar Documents. Ed. Austin Flannery. Fowler Wright Books Ltd., 1977

We do it for Jesus — Mother Teresa. E. Le Joly S.J. Darton, Longman and Todd, 1977

An excellent introduction to the process of Ignation spiritual discernment is *Eyes to See, Ears to Hear* by David Lonsdale S.J., detailed above—particularly see chapter 4.

An excellent introduction to the Jesus Prayer is *The Jesus Prayer* by Per-Olof Sjögren — written by a Lutheran Minister, translated by an Anglican; originally with a Foreword by a Catholic priest when first published in English by SPCK in 1975. Now published by Triangle in an edition of 1986, revised in 1996.

The Scripture quotations are from *The New Jerusalem Bible.* Darton, Longman & Todd, London, and Doubleday & Co., Inc., New York, 1985.